MW01241944

Create a Memoir - Leave a Legacy

CAPTURE LIFE

Write a Biography
Your Own or Someone Else's

How You Can Write a Life Story
Five Techniques to Get You Started
How You Can Publish the Story

Write!
Nikki Hanna

Nikki Hanna

Published by Patina Publishing
727 S. Norfolk Avenue
Tulsa, Oklahoma 74120
neqhanna@sbcglobal.net
www.nikkihanna.com

Copyright © 2012 by Nikki Hanna

IBSN: 978-0-9828726-3-5 (print)
ISBN: 978-0-9828726-6-6 (electronic)

Library of Congress Control Number: 2012900271

Manufactured in The United States of America

Thanks to Melanie Corbin, Laura Gordon, James Bethel, and Wayne Kruse for their contributions, to Toni Ellis and Terri Walker for their support and encouragement, to Donna Parsons for her advice and for championing me so enthusiastically, and to my grandchildren for thinking I am somehow cosmically important.

C O N T E N T S

INTRODUCTION: Why a Biography - 11

HOW TO WRITE A BIOGRAPHY

MECHANICS OF CREATING A BIOGRAPHY

PUBLISHING A BIOGRAPHY

INTRODUCTION

Life is transient. Unless a life story is captured, at some point it is lost forever. This suggests an urgency about the capture. Yet people delay recording their story or someone else's because they believe there is more of life to come and time to document it later. Maybe there is and maybe not. **Life is without a doubt tenuous.**

Others don't believe their life is important or interesting enough to chronicle and pass on. They are mistaken. A life story does not have to be a universally popular book appealing to the masses to be significant. There is an audience for every biography. This book reveals how to discover and describe the essence of a person and the wonder of the world in which they lived. It also shows how to do so in a way that others will want to read it. **Every life is remarkable in its own right and worthy of preservation.**

Some people don't document their story because they believe they cannot write. You don't have to be a writer. Just tell your story in your own words and in your own way. Those who know you will recognize your "voice" and appreciate the way you said things because it sounds like you. That means more than a professional writing job. This book facilitates the novice by introducing techniques and encouragement that nourish writing skills. **Everyone can write.**

While writing and self-publishing my auto-biography, I learned how to make a book happen. After finding the process fulfilling and the response of readers touching and rewarding, I was moved to encourage others to capture life stories. This book is the result, although I did not consciously set out to write it. That came about by accident.

> I made a proposal to a local college to teach a class on biographical writing. It was accepted. Developing the handouts, I was astounded to realize there was so much information to share that I easily had over a hundred pages. I was unintentionally writing a book about how to write a book. So I switched gears and began intentionally writing a book. This is the result.

Incorporated herein are the impressions and lessons learned from my autobiographical experiences. Readers are encouraged to supplement this "how to" information with their own perspectives, to learn from other sources, and to find their own approach to chronicling life. My way was to go full out and produce a book. This is not necessary. For many, a less intense approach is a better fit. It doesn't matter how you do it. The important thing is that you do it, that you capture life stories, yours or someone else's, while you still can.

My path included participating in writing seminars, classes at local universities, and reading books on creative writing, biographical writing, and publishing. This concentrated effort is not for everyone. However, a steep learning curve is part of the process of generating a beautiful life story. Whether you aggressively seek learning or not, you will learn from writing a biography, and that knowledge will be nourishing.

To encourage readers to add learning to their arsenal of tools used to record life, I share in this book my experiences in acquiring the knowledge required to become a better writer. More importantly, I introduce valuable techniques designed to get the novice writer started and to fulfill the promise that everyone can write.

This book is about telling a life story through the printed word. There are other wonderful methods. Videos and recordings communicate images and sounds not possible through writing, delivering unparalleled graphic details and liberal doses of visual and audio remembrances. Every medium has its place, each making its own unique contribution to portraying a life. No doubt a multi-medium approach is optimal for conveying the true essence of a person, each method complementing the other.

That said, let me make a case for the written word lest it get lost in the stampede toward technological solutions to everything. There is something special about a book--that tangible by-product of the written word that you can touch and feel, put down and pick back up, set on a coffee table or hand to someone you love, flip the pages, gaze at the pictures, and linger over the robust stories. Embellished with old photos and rich with writer narrative, there is simply nothing else like it.

A friend of mine made videos of conversations with his grandmother, put them on disks, and gave them as gifts. A wonderful gift, no doubt, but he could tell by talking to young relatives that they hadn't listened to it, at least not all of it. The young have many distractions. For different reasons, older generations are unlikely to access life stories in electronic form.

Perhaps young people won't read a book either, but it is not somewhere in an electronic cloud and it doesn't require equipment to access it. How many of us have tapes from old recorders that have deteriorated or we can't find a machine to play them on? A book is on a night stand, magazine rack, bookshelf, or coffee table as an enduring reminder of its presence--inviting, accessible, and ever so discoverable. When choosing your path to capturing life, consider the value of the written word.

My personal biographical journey may not be relevant to others. Everyone's path is unique, just as each life is remarkably different. Apply the particulars herein to the extent that they work for you, and where they don't, be courageous about doing your own thing. Your biography is your story or that of someone you care about. Make it a story as unique and fascinating as the life you are capturing.

There is a broad spectrum of approaches to producing a biography, with huge variances in intensity of effort. At one end is the simple, expedient approach of just getting stories on paper and out there for friends and family. The other end of the spectrum involves investing in the development of journalistic and publishing skills, stringing stories together into a comprehensive book, and marketing it.

Wherever you fit along this continuum, know that there is no right or wrong way to produce a life story. The important thing is that life is captured and shared. Sharing is what biography is about just as it is what life is about.

I use the experiences with my autobiography, *Out of Iowa,* herein to demonstrate how that book came to fruition, to reflect on the lessons learned while creating it, to share the immense rewards it produced, and to illustrate writing techniques. Don't assume you must go all out as I did. You can create a wonderful story without being "a writer" and without producing "a book." Do it your way, in your voice, on your level, and in whatever form is comfortable for you. By doing so, you will create something that is all kinds of crazy beautiful because it is uniquely yours.

> Because you captured your life or someone else's, grandchildren, future descendants, and others will have a sense of their heritage and the legacy of your work.
>
> They may never experience the time or place where their ancestor grew up, but they will know that place. They may never meet the person whose story you told, but they will know him or her because you captured life.
>
> **Through your writing, the past connects with the future, generations link together in a common thread, and a legacy is created.**

Capture life, write a biography, and share the story. It will live forever, and you will have given the gift of legacy.

- I -

HOW TO WRITE

A BIOGRAPHY

You may think: "I can't write."
The truth is: Everyone can write.

CHAPTER -1-

SETTING THE STAGE

Capturing a life story is a noble and reverent task. What can be more important than a person's life? A biography honors that life--that unique, meaningful, touching history of a life lived. This book provides a roadmap that will put anyone on the path to translating life into a story so compelling that everyone will want to read it. The big news is that anyone can write a biography, and that is the most important message of this book.

YOU CAN DO IT: With knowledge, time, motivation, and reasonable expectations on the level of performance, anyone can write a biography. (You don't have to build a Cadillac. A shiny Kia will do nicely.) **You are never going to have the perfect book. The important thing is that you have one.**

As my restless grandson said, while wiggling on his little behind, eagerly observing me struggling to assemble a toy or shifting on his feet as I'm on a stepstool stretching to reach food coloring for cookie frosting: "YOU can do it." This was not so much an expression of confidence as it was one of desperation, but his pleading emphasis on the "you" was motivating. YOU can do this. You can write about life. Read on and learn how.

VISION: It is important to understand why you are writing a biography and your goals in doing so. Whatever the reasons, define them. This assures they are realized in the end product. Articulate them vividly in your mind and honor them throughout the story development process. Keep your objectives always at the forefront.

Maybe you write because someone asked you to, or you do not want to die with your story still in you. Your goal might be to honor your family, delight elderly relatives, share wisdom, inspire generations to come, build family pride, simply create a record of family history, or all of these things. In the introduction to my memoir, *Out of Iowa,* I summarized my reasons for writing it.

With the encouragement of my daughter I decided to write this book. She said, "Do it for my kids. I want them to know where they came from and what it was like for you. I want them to know what you know." That was a compelling call to action and just the nudge I needed to retrace my early years, reflect on how they influenced the rest of my life, and record those recollections for future generations...

I am "Out of Iowa" and in a sense so are my grandchildren and any future descendants. They may never see Iowa, but they will know Iowa because I told my story. It is a good thing to know. Iowa is a wonderful place to grow up and a great place to be from. It is a part of me and of them. (*Out of Iowa,* p.13)

APPROACH: Everyone has a different vision and unique objectives for both the process of creating a biography and the end product. To accommodate as many objectives as possible along the continuum of approaches, information herein has been developed on two levels:

> **Method I**: Producing a book or booklet printed locally in small quantities and distributed to family and friends.

> **Method II:** Producing a commercial biography to be published, marketed, and sold through book distribution channels to a larger audience.

Whichever method is embraced, readers will find resourceful information herein to guide them through the processes--a roadmap for writing and producing a life story in booklet or book form. Producing a book is an ambitious project, and if you are not so inclined, consider applying the information herein to writing biographical short stories or journals, legacies in their own right.

PERSPECTIVE: Producing a biography can be overwhelming. If this book leaves you feeling as if you have been hit by a tsunami wave of information, think about the first day of a class when you got the syllabus for a semester's work. Recall how you thought you couldn't possibly do all those things, but when spread over the course of a four-month semester, they were considerably less intimidating and quite doable.

Writing a book is like that. It is intimidating at first blush, but by breaking it down into segments and spreading the work over time, it is achievable. Many things you must do are done once to build a base, and they never have to be done again. Don't let the details and action steps derail you from the amazing biography you aspire to create. Look down the road a year from now at all you will have accomplished and then imagine what you can do in several years.

One advantage of writing a biography is a flexible timeline. You may be on a steep learning curve if you are not a seasoned writer, but you get to set the time frames. Take years if you want and produce a quality book that will delight family and friends. Take breaks, set an easy pace, and enjoy the process.

The Urgency of Interviews: A compelling caveat to this casual time frame approach is this: Pursue interviews with a sense of urgency. You can develop the story later, but having a person-to-person conversation may not be possible down the road, especially if you are writing about an older person. Put interviews at the top of your

22

agenda. Take a *seize the moment* approach to gathering information from people.

> A friend of mine planned to take her seemingly healthy but elderly mother on a road trip to visit relatives, during which time she intended to probe for information for a possible life story. I met with her to encourage that effort and to advise her on interviewing techniques. The next day, her mother passed away. The story will get written, no doubt, but as is often the case, some speculation on details and personal perspectives will be required.

Writing and shaping what you write into a viable work takes time. Don't let this detract from uncovering the priceless gems that interviews expose--the things someone has never revealed before. You may know many facts about a person's life, but the feelings surrounding those facts and the words used to express them are the jewels of biography. **Don't delay. Do interviews early in the capturing of life process.**

One more note. When writing a life story, you are also writing that of others. Perhaps you don't write Mom's biography because she is gone, but write your own and include her story therein. Diane Keaton recently wrote her memoirs, *Then Again*, with emphasis on her mother's rich treasure of journals--a biography within a biography. No one's story is about just one life.

HINT: When gathering information from older people, ask about their parents and grandparents. Delve deeply into that history for every detail you can unearth. Most of these stories are already lost. Include what you discover in your story. The relevance may be more profound than you first imagined. What they did brought you to where you are today.

PURPOSE: Why write a biography? It is a rewarding, introspective, cathartic, bonding, and creative experience, but even more important, it can be incredibly inspiring to others. I found that inspiration years ago in the first autobiography I read, and I wrote about it in *Out of Iowa.*

...I read Bette Davis's autobiography. She faced tough times in her early career fighting the contract studio system in Hollywood, going through divorces, suffering abuse, and being financially devastated with children to support. Yet she persevered and rallied over and over. Her world and experiences were so foreign to me that I was mesmerized by them and, more importantly, how she coped with them. Her strength and fortitude were fascinating to me because my life had been so cushy.

My Iowa world consisted of stability and intense support systems. No woman would be left to her own devices in that world, and I never observed women with gumption. I saw strong women, but they got things done more by patience, persistence, and perhaps some degree of manipulation. Bette had moxie, faced problems head on, and took no crap. After my divorce, when my world got rather crazy, I often thought about her desperate struggles and how she ultimately prevailed. It was my only frame of reference for dealing with chaotic change and facing unknown challenges as an independent woman with limited resources and burdensome responsibilities. I drew on her experiences for inspiration and hope during that dark interlude and during other difficult times throughout my life. Another person's experiences, once shared through biography, can profoundly influence someone else's life. (Out of Iowa, p. 135)

The most appreciated compliments I received on my autobiography were from those who said it inspired them to capture a life story, to interview an elderly relative, to get busy and write some things down. Chronicling a life is a gift to others. You are re-gifting to generations a life with all its joyful and tragic experiences and myriad of lessons learned. Through biography, wisdom is shared, a life memorialized, and a legacy articulated. Any one of these alone is no small thing. Together they are transforming.

I sat at the feet of an uncle when he was in his final days while he captivated me with stories about World War II. He fought in three major battles in the Pacific. It was highly unusual for a soldier to be in all three battles and especially exceptional that he survived them. Confusion over his common name caused him to be shipped home by mistake and then redirected to the next major battle. When I mentioned this in passing to other relatives, I discovered they did not know about it. I found that amazing. It was such an extraordinary tale. My uncle was soon gone and I realized then the urgency of capturing a person's story. Once they are gone, it is lost forever.

People often think their life is not interesting, when in fact everyone's life is incredibly unique and intriguing in its own right, and everyone has a wealth of lessons learned in his or her head.

While writing my autobiography, I regurgitated a lot of information onto paper for the first draft-- uncensored, no holds barred. Then I began taking things out that I thought were not worthy of the final book, putting them in an *outtakes file.* My daughter read it and pleaded with me to put many of them back in the book.

One of the things I reluctantly reinstated was stories about chickens on the farm. Yes, chickens. To me experiences around chickens were trivial. To her they were quaint, amusing novelties. She contended that one day they would be fascinating to her urban children, who are unlikely to encounter free-range chickens.

What is ordinary to you now will be extraordinary to someone years from now. Here is a small sample of the chicken episodes in *Out of Iowa,* wonderful childhood stories I was prepared to throw away--stories that time will embellish with surprise and fascination.

Chickens ran free on the farm...In modern terms you could say they were free-range chickens. Everyone was constantly tiptoeing around chicken poop which was all over the place.

We went barefoot all summer. When we stepped in chicken poop it squished up between our toes which sent us scampering for the water pump.

Of all the animals on the farm, chickens were what captivated us kids the most. They were accessible. With a little effort you could catch one and carry it around or whatever. There was a lot of whatever going on. To small children, chickens were at the lowest end of the pecking order with us just one rung up. This was not true of the other animals. They could get the better of us, but chickens, well, they were fair game, except for a couple of roosters who periodically made it clear where we really stood in the farmyard order of things.

The roosters were mean and intimidating. They chased us when we were small, wings spread to make them appear larger, necks outstretched, beaks forward. Once my brother and I declared war on them. We put on layers and layers of clothes so they couldn't peck us, took up a garden hoe and rake and went rooster fighting. We may have believed we won, but we did hightail it for the front porch a couple of times with a raging rooster on our heels, garden tools abandoned in the dust...As we got older, the pecking order shifted and we could look at a threatening, mean-spirited rooster with considerable arrogance and say: "Really?"

Our hometown sponsored a pet parade as a community event. We had a couple of dogs and barn cats. With four brothers, all the real pets were spoken for, so I had to decide between a chicken and a baby pig. I chose the chicken, which was significantly quieter and somewhat easier to control than a squealing, twisting boar, at least so I thought.

Mom and I went out to the chicken house to pick out the hen to be my pet for the day. We selected an old one, thinking she would be mellow, overlooking the fact that she was excessively grumpy. Mom rigged up a basket for me to carry her in, dressed me in a bonnet and calico dress, and I carried "the little red hen" in the pet parade. Not being a real pet, the hen was not fond of the idea. Additionally, she was hungry. Chickens are always hungry. As I was struggling to load her into the basket, she spotted a mole on my neck, decided it was something to eat and pecked it off. (You can't make this stuff up.) I bled briefly, but was determined to be in the parade with my brothers, so I somehow wrangled her into the basket and kept her there long enough to get down the street in spite of her obvious and legitimate concerns about the proximity of several hyped-up bird dogs straining on their leashes.

After the parade Mom was wrestling with limited success to transfer the hen into the trunk of the car, a good time, I thought, to suggest that we eat her. Since she was an egg-laying hen and we kids had already murdered two of her compadres (one by a wanton brother with grand hunting delusions and a BB gun and another because of her inability to fly when thrown off a tall building), Mom made it clear that having her for supper was not an option. (*Out of Iowa*, pp. 59, 60)

This is only a flavor of a whole chapter of colorful free-range chicken tales ranging from hypnotizing them, raising and butchering hundreds of them, and tossing them off buildings to see if they could fly. Though these stories seem ordinary to me, they will no doubt be a novelty to my urban grandchildren. **If you think your life is not interesting, consider what was ordinary about your childhood that your descendants will never experience.**

THE REWARDS: Writing your life story, or that of others, is a solitary, introspective experience. You will spend many hours alone at your computer or with a note pad, but you will be enlightened and liberated, probably beyond your wildest dreams.

You will see yourself as a child, and perhaps for the first time view that child from an adult perspective. Tortured by the traumas and embarrassments and elated and inspired by the blessings, you will fall in love with that child. Feelings of deep compassion for all he or she endured will surface, and an unfamiliar vision of the endearing sweetness and innocence of that child will be revealed to you for the first time. As a result, you will view your adult self in a new light. This happens because you came to know the child through writing your story.

Furthermore, you will view your parents from an enlightened perspective. You have now played that role yourself and can finally authentically comprehend the challenges parenthood entails. You will see your parents as people, a fresh view beyond the narrow one of them as your source of nurturing.

Hopefully, you will come to realize that although they were not perfect, they did the best they could with what they had and what they knew. Although you may never know what their childhood was like or the demons they faced, traces of their struggles are revealed for the first time as you thoughtfully contemplate their lives. A sense of mercy and tenderness may be introduced through your fresh interpretation of them as products of their environment. Their contributions to your life will be seen with renewed clarity, and you will appreciate more the sacrifices made. Perhaps you will thank them.

The impact of grandparents, siblings, aunts, uncles, teachers, and others transforms from fuzzy memories into revelations of their imprint on the person you became.

To realize healing enlightenment, you must expand memories beyond the facts of what happened and enter the realm of feelings. It is not the events, but how you and others felt about them that makes them important. As you resurrect memories, resurrect the feelings around them. How did you feel when you read your mother's funeral arrangements and the last instruction was: "You kids take care of each other"? What do you think she was feeling when she wrote it?

You will discover themes in your life you didn't know existed--the threads running through it that manifest themselves in behavior and choices. As a consequence, you come to realize what makes you tick and understand why and how you became the person you are today. You discover the essence of your individuality.

In addition to your own personal growth, others will benefit from your biographical journey. Once my autobiography was published, I saw the joy it brought to others. Friends were entertained and inspired by the accomplishment. Those close to me understood me better and could relate much of my life to their own.

Siblings and classmates from my generation resurrected their own memories from the escapades and exploits of my youth, and we reconnected. I was surprised to realize the value my biography held for nieces, nephews, cousins, and other young people who enjoyed the details of their parents' youth and appreciated what I thought were rather preachy lessons learned. Much to my surprise, several of my son's buddies at Owasso's Fishbonz Pool Hall bought copies after asking: "Is Marty in there?"

Neighbors and others in the town where I grew up were delighted. Young people bought the book for their parents and parents for their children. (Biographies make great gifts for anniversaries, birthdays, and holidays.) I was contacted by people I'd not heard from in years.

> One of the childhood stories I recounted in *Out of Iowa* was about the custom of leaving May Baskets on people's front porches on May 1. We yelled "May Basket" and ran like crazy to the car while children burst out of houses or appeared from hiding places to chase us down and kiss us.
>
> On May 1, fifty-some years later, UPS delivered a May Basket to my porch from a

childhood friend who had recently read my biography. If I had realized soon enough what was in the package, I would have surely followed tradition and chased down a horrified delivery man and kissed him.

Some consequences were totally unexpected. I noted in the book that personal trainers, Danny and Levi, tried to kill me, but that they were cute in the process. They wanted copies--probably because I called them cute.

My therapist, who had earlier invested in drawing me out of a post-retirement depression, told me she was "reveling in my awesomeness." It doesn't get any better than that.

To my amazement, everyone wanted their book autographed. I felt awkward about this at first but flattered and willing once I adjusted to the idea. There were numerous wonderful outcomes from producing my biography, but the most important one was that a curious and unexpected sense of relief and peace set in. **I knew I would not die with my story still in me.**

TIME FRAME: How long will it take to write a biography? However long you want it to take. I recently asked an author how long it took to write his book, and he said five years. Another seasoned author knocked one out in six months. You can churn and churn and never let go of one.

At some point, you've got to cut it off and get it out. Still, you get to decide when that happens.

After working a year on my book, I was encouraged by a writing class instructor to stop churning and send it to print. I took his advice and regretted it. More polish would have made it much better. However, this is a never-ending reality. You will constantly be noting opportunities to enhance the book.

If you have this experience, the good news is that once it is printed, you can polish it up and print better copies later. On the other hand, you can churn forever and never go to print. It is a challenge to know when a book is "cooked," especially since you are eager to share it.

HINT: To avoid the temptation to rush a book out prematurely, share a draft copy with people you trust. I gave drafts to my brothers the day of my mother's funeral and collected them later when the book came out. (I didn't want the drafts floating around for years or discovered in someone's attic. As your book evolves, you will be embarrassed by earlier drafts. This is a sign of progress. You wouldn't want the opposite reaction.)

Unless you have written a book before, you are going to be on a steep learning curve for quite some time. Allow enough time to incorporate into your finished product the knowledge you acquire during the process. Take time to produce a quality biography that will shine for generations. Just remember, it does not have to be a professional book. It just needs to reflect a life lived, its lessons, uniqueness, and the subtleties that make the person who he is.

It took a year to write *Out of Iowa.* I was retired with time to invest. It would have taken many times that if I had been working. During this time, I went to seminars, read books, researched online, and took computer classes. All that accumulated knowledge was factored into the book. Sometimes I wrote all day and deep into the night. Occasionally, I took breaks from the intensity of it.

> **HINT: Periodically put the manuscript away for awhile. A fresh perspective will present itself when you return to it, and considerable polish will result.**

Invest whatever time is required to do a good job and to allow yourself to enjoy the process.

DEFINITION OF SUCCESS: As the book evolves and you accumulate the skills required to produce it, you may begin to think about marketing it. Doing so is probably much more complex than you imagine and should not be entered into lightly. You'll understand why when you read the rest of this book. In the meantime, it is helpful to ask yourself some questions.

Do you want to simply capture life and share it with others, or do you aspire to become a professional writer? Is it important to make money by selling a book? As you become educated in the immense challenges of being successful financially at writing, defining success by something other than book sales and financial outcomes manages expectations and tempers the intensity of disappointments.

Making money or even recovering the cost of producing a book is a formidable challenge. Pursue your dreams but do this: **Define success simply as having created the book and shared it with those who are interested. Success is guaranteed at that level. You can do that.**

Be courageous in finding your own path. Brace yourself for penetrating introspection. Be prepared to be overwhelmed and to adjust to the fluid nature of the process. Do these things and you will experience some kind of wonderful from the biographical experience, and you can share that with others.

Achieving that requires a concerted effort and significant determination. There will be challenges, some of the most common of which you will discover in the next chapter. Remember that when trials surface and the spirit wavers: **YOU can do it.**

Chapter -2-

CHALLENGES

There are a number of challenges to producing a biography and many of them will present themselves immediately. Recognizing them up front removes the shock factor and mitigates their impact somewhat, although they will still challenge the spirit. Remain determined and don't let obstacles deprive you of your goals.

> **HINT: When becoming discouraged with the magnitude of the task of producing a biography, don't focus on what you don't know or what is challenging in the moment. Look back and contemplate how far you have come, what you have learned, and all that you have accomplished.**

TECHNOLOGY: A certain amount of technical skill is required to produce a book. This was a curse to me. I was spending a fortune on geeks and was continuously frustrated. Finally, I just gave up. Technical problems frequently brought me to tears, and it became too emotionally draining to endure. My goal was to write books when I retired, and I couldn't pull it off.

This was devastating and led to depression--a vague, chronic emptiness. Unable to realize my dream of writing books, I ended up in therapy. I felt like a dinosaur, as if I didn't fit in the world anymore, and I couldn't master doing the things I always wanted to do. That was a loss.

My counselor recommended a peculiar treatment plan. I was to get an Apple computer and sign up for the support package, giving me access to trainers and project support. That single piece of advice made me an author and changed what I call "my encore years." With my user friendly Apple *MacBook* laptop, I was back in the game. I could do some stuff.

Determined and hell-bent, I installed an Apple computer, a wireless thingy, and a printer all by myself in just six hours with only nine help desk calls. I was a high-tech momma, let me tell you. One of the calls to the help desk was to report missing cords. The young fellow was very nice. After a long and pregnant pause, he said, "IT IS WIRELESS." I said, "Okay, thank you." (*Out of Iowa*, p. 235)

Not only did I write books, I included photos, designed covers, sales brochures, bookmarks, business cards, and developed a website. Had I anticipated doing all this when I started out, I would have been intensely intimidated, but one by one and over time each found its spot on the agenda, and all got done. This did not happen overnight, but it did take place within a year and a half. Imagine where I will be in a few years.

This was accomplished only because I could take my laptop to the Apple store and the wonderful children there helped me. I refer to them as children affectionately. They are responsible, mature adults, but two generations behind me, so I can't help but consider them children--lovely, sharp, accommodating little geniuses who patiently and determinedly nursed me through the learning required to accomplish my goals.

An unexpected bonus emerged from this affiliation. For the first time in years, I felt connected to the younger generation. I recently helped one of them with his business class homework. I do what I can. A help desk kid asked me if I had my cookies activated. I called him a rascal. As I said, I love the Apple children. I also love the Apple store. With all its chaos and pulsating activity, which is normally irritating to a person of my age, it evolved into my happy place. I did amazing things there which I never could have imagined.

If you are not a technical genius, you are going to be severely challenged to get a book out unless you have someone to support you in the technical area. Don't wait to resolve this problem to begin writing. Go ahead and get started. Write on a tablet or whatever works for you, but know that at some point you will need technical skills to pull off a book. If you can't bring yourself to embrace technology on that level, seek a collaborator.

A Technical Challenge in *Out of Iowa*

Here's a feature for you. The MacBook has a little dot at the top of the screen which is a camera. I did not know this, so it was quite a shock at one point in the installation process to suddenly see myself pop up on the screen, large as life, in my jammies, hair askew and no makeup. The angle was not good. It showed my neck, for god's sake, made my nose look big, and the lighting was horrible. Worst of all, there was cleavage, which generated severe panic, the kind that sets off the fight or flight response. I was on the world-wide web with cleavage and looking like crap...I was panic stricken. (You can't make this stuff up.) So, I rushed back to the bathroom to fix up in order to appeal to the more discriminating males.

After regrouping, I adjusted the screen for a better angle, softened the lighting, and reported the problem to a help desk child who assured me that no one saw it but me. "But I'm all fixed up now," I said. Anyway, I now have tape over the little dot which is a camera. I just don't trust it. My computer is in the kitchen, and someone might see me loading the dishwasher naked...(*Out of Iowa*, p. 235)

Computer Backup: Pay special attention to computer backup. I can't think of anything worse than losing an entire book because of a technical failure. Almost every writer has a horror story about losing important work. Have someone help, if you must, but set up a solid backup capability and routinely verify that it is working.

HINT: Periodically attach your work to an email and send it to yourself. This gets it out there in the internet cloud. Also, print it occasionally and keep the latest iteration of a hard copy in a fireproof safe or another location. (You need to print periodically anyway to proof and edit from hard copy.) You can also copy the manuscript onto a flash drive and put it in a safe place. I do all of these things periodically.

LEGAL ISSUES: This is scary because even if you have done nothing wrong, people can still sue you. You should prevail in the end, but you do have to deal with the lawsuit. Every time I went to a writing class and the instructor talked about legal issues, I became so concerned about the consequences that I gave up on publishing a book. But who wants to die with their book still in them because of lawyers? Eventually, I'd get back in the saddle and soldier on.

HINT: Don't avoid writing about risky topics. Getting them down on paper provides a hedge against senility and gets things off your chest. (Juicy topics are the ones that hold a fascination for descendants. Remember *Bridges of Madison County*.) Write with abandon. Just don't publish the dicey stuff--yet. *Some day you may be poor enough and old enough to*

publish without risk. More about this later in the discussion of the first draft.

If your biography is limited to close family and friends and you are gentle with people, if you focus on the good in others, verify facts, consider other people's perspectives, and keep the story positive, you can most likely dodge any legal bullets. **Be cognizant of potential legal implications, but don't let the fear of legal consequences keep you from capturing life.**

> In writing my biography I focused on the growing up years--family oriented subjects such as nurturing, relationships, generation gaps, aging, and how the early Iowa years affected the rest of my life. I avoided, or at least danced around, the spicy subjects of unfortunate romances, crazy friends making bad decisions, and a career rife with men who interpreted my presence as an invasion of sacred territory. This reduced legal risks for now, but someday I will write about those things. They are too fascinating not to share.

Changing names and enough other information so no one can tell who people are provides some legal protection, but that is nearly impossible to accomplish. (If you do so, disclose that in the introduction.) You can also write a biography as fiction and substantially change everything, but that seems to defeat the purpose of capturing a life story. If your goal is a memoir, you're probably not inclined to want to write fiction--a whole different animal. Then there is always the question of whether you changed it enough to avoid legal action. You can never be sure of that.

You can always find a publishing attorney to advise you, or possibly scare the pa-hoot out of you and take your money in the process. Perhaps you simply write your story, be sensible about it, and let the chips fall where they may.

I am cognizant of legal risks, but I'm not going to let them prevent me from doing the writing I enjoy. Otherwise, I'd be back in the therapist's chair. You will have to decide the level of risk and caution appropriate for your situation.

RIGHTS AND REFERENCES: Another legal category that requires reflection is copyrights.

Rights: Never use song titles or lyrics of songs, not even a well-known birthday song, without permission. (Notice I didn't use a song name here.) They are typically copyrighted and song writers are particularly protective of their work.

Technically, you should have a release from any living person who is in a photo in your book.

Photographers and others can own the rights to photos, in which case you must get their permission to use them. You must also give the owner credit. Get a signed release. (Most old photos are not protected.)

HINT: Have a professional photographer take pictures of you that make you look "authory" and put one on the back cover of every book you write. Get a release from him that allows you to use the pictures any way you want without having to give him credit.

Some art, statues, monuments, buildings and other structures are protected. Even if you take a picture of them yourself, you cannot publish it without a release. In a book I'm writing, I am including a picture of me looking at a painting. I contacted the painter and got a release. However, the painting is owned by someone else, so to be safe, I'll seek his permission as well.

References: If you quote more than two sentences from what someone else published, get their permission. If it is under two sentences, quote them but reference the work. Don't use someone else's published words without giving them credit. If you have a question whether something is a quote from someone else, you can often find the source of it through a search engine like Google.

Some written words are so commonly used that they become "public domain" and no one can own them. You can put words into a search engine and research whether something is all over the place without reference. If so, it is probably safe to use.

Authors are known to say something like: "Somebody, I'm not sure who, said..." probably because they were unable to find the source and just had to include the remark. Many common phrases and statements are impossible to trace.

> **HINT: If you have concerns about whether something is copyright protected, just don't use it. Find another way to communicate your thought. Most any writing problem can be solved by "writing around it." Write it a different way and make the reference issue moot.**

TONE: The tone of a book is a critical part of the biographical journey. This has to do with how things are said as well as what is included and what is left out. It is important to deliberately contemplate how the overall spirit of the book will impact others. Perhaps you don't care and can write with wild abandon, but that should be a conscious decision. Most likely you do care, in which case tone is fundamental.

> It is often said in the publishing industry that to be an interesting biographical writer you must be willing to kill your own

grandmother. Another thought is that there are some things you shouldn't write about until your parents are dead.

These statements may be true if you are going to be indiscriminate and insensitive about what you write and how you say it. There are plenty of examples of famous people revealing hurtful and embarrassing things about others in the interest of creating a provocative biography that will sell a large number of books. Don't do that. You don't necessarily have to leave out the ugly things. Creative writing can often make them colorful, humorous, or at least relatable. Once a writer determines the tone of the book, it governs what is included and the words used to tell about it.

You don't have to write about everything. Omission is an okay choice. There is no rule that says your book must be comprehensive. It's your book, and you get to decide what is in it. Use this writing opportunity to create an inspirational legacy. Most people did the best they could with what they had and what they knew. Make the unfortunate incidents humorous, tell about them compassionately, turn them into lessons learned, or leave them out.

HINT: Think about this: If you hurt someone with words, you hurt everyone around them.

Define in your mind what you want to accomplish by writing the book. If you want to make someone pay for making your life miserable, if you need to vent and get things off your chest, or your goal is to assign blame and seek consolation, then the tone will be negative. It is hard to imagine any good coming out of that scenario, and if those are your objectives, you may want to retain a lawyer.

> **HINT: If it makes you feel better, go ahead and transfer your issues and bitterness onto paper in the interest of "getting it all out." Be as harsh and direct as you like. This is good therapy. Just don't publish those words. Soften the edges for the book. Consider the tragedy of people's lives that caused them to do the things they did. It is healing to take unfortunate events and portray them in clever, sympathetic ways.**

Everyone has had hard times and has experienced some degree of abuse at the hands of another. Each of us can choose to assume a victim role and fill a book with stories of persecution and trials. On the other hand, we can paint inspirational pictures of life's challenges by reflecting on ways we and those we write about overcame the harsh realities of life.

By demonstrating an appreciation of the demons others faced, a negative history is portrayed with hope and promise. A good example of this is *Angela's Ashes* by Frank McCourt, who experienced a nightmarish childhood. If he can write a compelling but sympathetic book given his horrific history, anyone can. His resilience is a tonic for damaged children and a cathartic remedy for parents who were the casualty of their own unfortunate history. Search for that history about yourself and others. Dig deep.

When viewing toxic adults as hurt children-- victims of their own difficult past--a sense of compassion and empathy is reflected in the words you choose to describe them.

It is highly likely that by writing a biography you will offend or embarrass someone, whether intending to or not. Bummer. Interviewing the players and considering their perspectives can mitigate this prospect and enrich your book with diverse viewpoints. There is an incredible degree of latitude when putting a spin on a story. Be compassionate, take the high road, and be gentle with people--go for an upbeat, hopeful tone.

An autobiography can take on a tone of self-indulgence. In the first draft, include all your amazing qualities and accomplishments, but as you shape the book in subsequent drafts, consider what is really relevant to readers. Don't turn them off with a brag fest. Conversely, you can be too hard on yourself in which case your book reflects a victim mentality and takes on a negative, un-inspirational tone. Don't ignore the mistakes, hurts, and vulnerabilities. They are what make you human, but focus on how you overcame them and moved on.

UNWILLING KEY PLAYERS: Interest is aroused when news spreads that you are writing a memoir. There may be people who adamantly don't want you to write about them. It's a free country, and if you stick to the truth and are prepared for the consequences, you can say whatever you like.

Amazingly, when you don't write about them, these same people feel left out. When people insist that they don't want to be in your book, consider leaving them out. Write around them. This might be an obvious omission that readers puzzle over, but it was their choice, not yours. If it is crotchety old Aunt Madge, your book probably won't suffer. If it is Dad, well, that's another story.

> **HINT: If people vital to your story indicate they don't want you to write about them, do it anyway. Portray them in a delightful way, and let them read the draft. Invite them to contribute. Odds are they will change their mind. If not, brace**

for the consequences or take them out of the book.

It is not unusual for people to worry about what you are saying when they discover a book is in progress. Share passages and seek their input. When they see what you've written, they might become your biggest champions. By involving them, you may discover another story you knew nothing about and perhaps even another chapter for the book.

INTERVIEWING TECHNIQUES: Whether writing about your life or someone else's, you will be interviewing people. This may be like pulling teeth. Let's say you are writing about your mom and she gives you short, curt answers, claims she can't remember anything, or she can't imagine that anything she has to say matters.

Get her in a car and take her on road trips, preferably to visit other elderly friends and relatives whom you can interview. During car time, ask her questions followed by more questions. For example, a conversation with a woman in her eighties might go like this:

"Mom, who was your best friend in school?"

"Pearl."

"What was Pearl like?"

"She was smart and fun."

"What else?"

"She lived down the road in a rent house. We walked back and forth. When cars passed, the dust choked us. I could run faster than Pearl. I could run faster than anyone in my school."

"What did you and Pearl do for fun?"

"We went to church and slumber parties. We played Monopoly. I always beat her. She borrowed too much money."

"What did you do at slumber parties?"

"We rolled our hair with rags to make Shirley Temple curls, and Mom made us popcorn with chocolate on it. Her mom and dad fought a lot, and I didn't like staying there. Her brother got beat up. We hid in the closet with Skeeter. Pearl cried. I didn't. She kept hugging me. Skeeter licked us. I didn't tell Mom."

"Why not?"

"I was afraid she wouldn't let me see Pearl anymore. We were like sisters."

"What did you like most about Pearl?"

"She was my best friend and we shared secrets. I could tell her things. We talked for hours. We shared clothes and played duets on the piano. We were like sisters."

"Is there anything you didn't like about her?"

"She was a redheaded spitfire and stole my boyfriends. I really didn't like her."

"Really? When did you last see Pearl?"

"She got polio and didn't graduate. They moved away. I don't know what happened to her. Some people were in iron lungs, you know."

"How did you feel about that?"

"I missed her, but I didn't cry. I didn't know what to do when she got sick. Mom wouldn't let me visit her because she was afraid of polio. I wondered why Pearl got it and not me. Maybe she got it swimming in the pond with her brother. I didn't like swimming in the pond. My feet would get stuck in the mud. My teacher got polio. She had one leg smaller than the other and wore a brace. I got a boyfriend, your dad, and got married after graduation. Everyone shivareed us."

"Shivareed?"

"People drove in our driveway honking horns and hollering. They brought food and drinks, and we had a party. We saw the headlights coming from down the road and knew we were in for it. Cousin Donnie got drunk, drove in a ditch, and got stitches in his head."

Imagine where two or three hours of asking questions can lead. Google shivaree and polio. Ask other relatives about them. Contradictions like the love/hate relationship with Pearl are revealing and worth exploring. Draw out details about those boyfriends and the romance with Dad. Who knows what other mischief cousin Donnie got into if he was known to drive down both sides of the road at the same time. Keep probing. Incredible stories can be constructed from nuggets like these.

Dig deep for descriptions, details, and how the person felt about things. Feelings are where the rich stories reside, and from them the essence of a person emerges. Jot down notes as soon as you can or use a recorder. Always have questions in mind that will draw the person out.

> **HINT: A national project to instruct and inspire people to record each other's stories has a list of *question generators* available on the website, *storycorps.org.* These questions are designed to elicit enticing details from a reluctant interviewee and to inspire story telling.**

EMOTIONAL ROLLER COASTER: One day you will feel your in-process biography is a brilliant, hilarious, captivating piece of literature and the next day it is, in your mind, rubbish. You will vacillate between pride and embarrassment. At times you will be certain everyone will view the end result as your folly.

When writing your autobiography, you will inevitably feel unpleasantly self-absorbed at times. It is all about "me, me, me," which doesn't feel good and may derail your efforts. You will wonder who cares about your life anyway. Well, you do. Please know that your life is important, that you matter. Write for yourself on the first draft. Then, in subsequent drafts, introduce a reader perspective that softens the edges of any blatant self-indulgence.

You also may have to struggle with family and relationship issues while writing the book, just as you do in life. Emotions surface, some over things you could not have anticipated. Fortunately, resurrecting feelings at this stage of life with the enlightenment of experience and maturity is healing.

There are a multitude of potential emotional distractions and interferences. When the roller coaster takes you to the bottom, take a break and talk to someone who champions your efforts. My daughter wanted my book to be written so badly that she kept me going many times. A brother reminded me my life was relevant. A good friend kept telling me my writing had promise.

The roller coaster continues after the book is written. As time passes, you will view earlier writings with embarrassment. This is good news. It means you are progressing. If you don't look back at your freshman effort and feel that you could have done better, you are not learning and growing as an author. Ride the roller coaster.

AUTHOR TRAUMAS: When you write about life, there will be traumas that spark regret and cause you to question why you are doing it. Low moments occur when it is discovered that something you wrote hurt someone in a way you had not anticipated, when you realize a publishing requirement was not met or a referencing requirement violated, or when errors are discovered after the book is printed. When traumas strike, acknowledge that there will be ups and downs. It is all worth it. Life is like that, and so goes your book.

WRITING CONFIDENCE: To many, the most formidable challenge to creating a biography is that voice in their head that says: "I can't write." That is so not true. Writing is putting words together. Everyone can write. You will learn how in Chapter 4 where newfound confidence is inspired by *five key techniques* and an abundance of other writing tips. They provide the writing novice with a framework that unleashes the skill everyone possesses. Apply these tips and you will discover this: **You can write.**

KEEPING TRACK: One of the challenges of writing a memoir is keeping track of those fleeting memories and ideas that pop into your head. You cannot deal with them in the moment, but you don't want to lose them either. Perhaps you are not ready to write about them yet or you're busy doing something else. If you don't capture them immediately, they are gone. Carry a note pad at all times. Set up a file or box in which to drop notes or keep a list. As you develop the manuscript, work in these thoughts.

HEARTBREAK: Writers are not naturally tough-skinned, but we need to be. Anne Lamott, a best selling author, had twenty-seven bad reviews in a row on one of her books, but she rallied and kept going. If you write a biography, someone will criticize it, but, hey, you wrote something. That's killer. Toughen up.

I hesitated to put these potential challenges in the early part of this book for fear of discouraging the tentative writer, but you need to know what is coming. Don't let the challenges dissuade you. They are only a small nuisance part of the process of capturing life. There are immense rewards, personal growth, and confidence awaiting the bravehearted. Yes, confidence. Once you write a biography, you will know that: **You can write**. That is no small thing. The next chapters show you how.

Chapter -3-

GETTING STARTED

To get started, just begin writing. Don't let anything hold you back. Make it a priority while simultaneously working on the other things required to produce a biography. There are many "other things." Here are some of them.

LEARNING: The best way to learn to be a writer is to write, and the way to become a better writer is to write. You don't have to be a seasoned writer to create a biography. An amateur effort has its own charm. Be prideful about whatever quirky, delightfully flawed narrative you produce.

If you aspire to a more polished outcome, put learning on your agenda and cultivate writing skills. Read biographies and "how to" books on writing in general and memoirs in particular. Read all kinds of books. You will get inspiration from every one. Writers read.

Take adult writing classes at colleges. The instructors are established authors, giving you access to seasoned experts who may critique portions of what you write--an awesome opportunity. Attend meetings of local writing groups. Search the web for connections and resources. Read writers' blogs.

> **HINT: Spend time in book stores and libraries perusing biographies. Review tables of contents. Examine the style, tone, and flavor of narratives. Read introductions. Note formats and use of photos. Analyze titles and subtitles. Study marketing techniques on covers, and read reviews. Observe how titles fit on the spines and whether they compete effectively for attention on the shelves. Purchase a few biographies. Read them and critique them.**

Seek information and factor acquired knowledge into the book's working drafts as you add wave after wave of polish to the biography. All the while, continue interviewing and writing.

TECHNICAL TOOLS: One of the most notable challenges of producing a book is the technical component. Technology is also the most amazing blessing, and it is essential to printing a book.

There are numerous technical requirements involved in producing a book. Efficiently setting up the text document, organizing it, formatting it, meeting printing standards, and inlining photos are all things you or someone assisting you must do. You will need to know how to save, back up, format, print, and transmit the files you create. All this happens through the use of technical tools. It may seem implausible that you can learn how to do all that, but step by step and over time, YOU can do it.

In addition, technology is required for research activities. Search engines like Google and Wikipedia are valuable sources of information on punctuation, grammar, spelling, verification of facts, determining references and finding quotes, identifying and researching vendors, locating websites, and a host of other components that facilitate the writing process. Familiarize yourself with them. These search capabilities are so valuable that you will find yourself using them for many things beyond writing activities. Efficient and comprehensive access to information will enhance your world.

SETTING UP: At some point, you must apply formatting capabilities to the draft. You can take time to set it up before you start writing, but that is not required. Any drafted information can be converted into the required format later. Formatting details are covered in *Chapter 5 - Writing Mechanics.*

Keep in mind that your overriding priorities throughout the biographical development

process are interviewing and writing. Don't put them off to learn formatting or anything else. When you are in the mood to write, write. When you have access to people, interview.

SCHEDULE AND TIMELINES: To stay motivated, you may need to schedule designated writing times. Reserve a couple of hours a day, or so many a week for writing. Set goals like a certain number of pages per sitting or a chapter a week. Writing at the same time every day can be helpful. Not everyone needs this structure. Some writers require discipline to keep from becoming so engaged that they write all day and night. Do what works. Consider deadlines flexible. If they stress you, adjust them.

To facilitate monitoring and controlling the biographical process, an action plan for producing a book is included in the *Appendix*. Attaching dates to such a plan keeps you on task, promotes progress, and measures results. Modify the plan to fit your goals. Don't let action plan details pressure you. The sheer number of steps is intimidating. View the plan as something reflecting how far you have come as well as what you must accomplish going forward.

PLACE TO WRITE: It is helpful to set up a place to write; however, it can be productive to write in many places.

HINT: Carry ear plugs in your purse or pocket. Poor acoustics and intrusive loud music are trendy in restaurants and public places. Additionally, you will inevitably be seated next to robust revelers, a person whose voice carries like a NASA blast off, or a parent who responds to whining and screaming with the positive payoff of more Cheerios. I love, love, love my ear plugs, the best invention since a suitcase with handles.

Take your laptop to a restaurant or coffee shop and sit there for hours. When traveling, writing is a welcome diversion in someone's guest room and in hotels, airport cafes, and on planes.

About the writing--this is the fun part, the act of creating. Let's talk about writing. Let the fun begin...

Chapter -4-

YOU CAN WRITE

EVERYONE CAN WRITE: For many, the actual writing of a life story is so intimidating that they are certain they cannot pull it off. The truth is that any reasonably educated person can put words together, one after the other, forming sentences that evolve into paragraphs, which then blossom into a story. Simply stated: **Those who believe they can't write, can.**

FIVE WRITING TECHNIQUES: Here are five techniques that will get even the most reluctant and timid potential author started.

> 1 - Break It Down
> 2 - Apply Layers
> 3 - Mine Tidbits
> 4 - Discover Defining Moments
> 5 - Expose Rebel Jewels

These techniques will turn you into a biographical writer, someone who beautifully and expressively captures life and shares it. Get out a notebook or computer. You are about to become a writer.

Technique 1
BREAK IT DOWN

Write incrementally. Don't focus on the whole book in the early stages of writing a life story. It will overwhelm you. Break it down into increments. Sitting down to write a biography, or any book for that matter, is an intimidating situation. Sitting down to write a short story about an episode in someone's life is less formidable. Write story by story.

> In her book *bird by bird* (the best book I've read on how to write), Anne Lamott tells how her brother was struggling with a school assignment to write about birds. His father, a writer, told him to just take it bird by bird.

A biography can be written subject by subject, event by event, emotion by emotion, story by story. In other words, write in increments. Take something--an incident, an emotion, a person, a character flaw, a time period, a romance, a soldier coming home, a pet, or whatever--and devote yourself to it. Focus on it, develop details, embellish, describe, frame, string words together, build phrase after phrase and sentence after sentence. Grow it into a story through description. Paint it with words. Stay with it. Don't leave it alone until it is a robust story. If you get stuck, jump ahead and write the ending. Then return to round out the story.

Then take another incident, possibly totally unrelated, and construct it. Then another, and another. Eventually, you will string these self-contained stories together, arrange them logically, link them with transitions, and make sense out of them. In the meantime, break it down into short stories.

HINT: Keep a list of potential stories as memories surface and work each one story by story.

Write about whichever topic appeals to you at that time--whatever suits your fancy. Follow your gut. When the mood strikes and something comes to mind, wherever you are and whatever you are doing, write it down. Go wherever your mind takes you. Flow with it. Keep building, heaping on details, revealing emotions, and creating a vivid image for the reader. Even life's minor interludes are rich with latent messages. Ferret them out and make them an integral part of a story. Later you will find a place for that story as the book is molded.

Anne Lamott has a radiant, descriptive way of painting pictures with words. Reading her words will inspire you to be a better writer. Worth observing are her self-deprecating humor which sympathetically exposes human flaws (a great tactic for an autobiography) and her use of metaphor and simile (techniques that turn stories into vivid pictures). If you read one book about writing, read Lamott's.

Her book is somewhat intimidating because we can only hope to be as good as she, but it will make you a better writer. The queen of metaphor, like Bonnie Raitt is the queen of slide, Lamott models expressive, entertaining writing. Like her father advising her young brother to write bird by bird, she will get you started, story by story, and you will discover that: **You can write**.

Technique 2
APPLY LAYERS

Layering is a simple three-step process that facilitates writing on a level deeper than mere description. First, write down a *fact,* an incident in the history of the person. Next, jot down *details* around that fact. Then explore the *feelings* people had about the incident. Finally, write with abandon about these things. This is where the magic happens. The result is a story-- one with interest and depth. It is as simple as that. Here are examples of this approach:

> Mom stated that she and Dad got engaged in 1940--a simple *fact*. When pressed for details,

she revealed that Dad bought her engagement ring for $10 after working many hours scooping manure and spreading it on the fields of a neighbor's farm to earn the money to pay for it--one of several interesting *details* around the fact. When asked about how she felt about getting engaged, she said she was irritated that they ran into a couple they knew as they left the jewelry store. It disturbed her that the pair would gossip about the engagement. This reflected her intensely private nature--a *feeling* about the event which was uniquely hers. Most young girls would have excitedly showed off their diamond. Delving into those feelings reveals the essence of a person.

When Dad was a boy, his older brother died--a *fact*. Interesting *details* around that event were that penicillin had not been discovered yet. The brother was kicked in the leg by a horse, developed an infection in the wound, and it overtook him. Enduring the torturous death of this young boy was traumatic for the entire family and wounded Dad deeply. Later, Mom and Dad lost three babies. The scars from these losses became vividly clear when Dad cautioned my brother, who was playing with his toddler, not to get too attached to her because he could lose her. Dramatically reflecting the depth of Dad's *feelings* around his personal losses and the degree to which they shaped him, this comment is a biographical treasure.

Whole chapters with great depth and detail can be developed around such information. Apply the process of layering facts, details, and, most of all, feelings around events and characters in a person's life and intriguing stories will evolve which any novice can mold into a splendid biography. **You can write.**

Technique 3
MINE TIDBITS

Capturing a life story is not about things of biblical proportions. You are not contemplating the world situation or the nature of the universe. Take a little thing, a tidbit, and grow it into a story. Concentrate on a feeling, a mood, an incident and write about it in vivid, expansive detail. Let the thoughts flow. Imagine.

Describe depression as a vague emptiness and then portray what that is like, and on and on. Characterize bliss, how someone found it, and what it meant to that person and others. Relationships between living things are rich with opportunities to elaborate. It does not have to be a story about Lassie. It can be a fleeting relationship, with or without a deep connection.

I described in my biography captivating tales about interactions with chickens on the farm, an unlikely topic at first blush, but one teeming with abundant details when explored rigorously. Those were not deep connections. I have never been "at one" with a chicken, but I have been "at one" with Coco, the squirrel living in a flower pot on my balcony with whom I commune daily. He eats the nuts I put out for him while I drink my morning coffee. I could write a chapter about Coco, his stretching routine when he exits his nest each morning, his uninhibited begging, his response to toast crusts and popcorn as surprising entrees, his rather hysterical confusion when I moved his flower pot a few feet to get it out of the rain, and his ungrateful detachment once he is fed.

It will be quite a story if he turns out to be a girl and baby squirrels scamper on my lawn chairs next spring, neighborhood cats circling below. The extent to which I would go to protect them is reflected in the peculiar efforts I've taken to defend his flower pot from the weather. Few squirrels have R-30 value insulation and an umbrella. I could go on and on. There is a story there, not one of epic proportions, but instead one that is a telling reflection of the person in that story--a consummate rescuer.

Interviews are rich with tidbits. Mom's intense desire for privacy reflected in the engagement ring incident inspired several references in my biography including this one about her funeral:

Intensely private, Mom was always insistent that she didn't want any kind of service when she died, so we kids, Aunt Weezie, and a few others simply gathered at the gravesite. Brother Kelly performed a short non-service during which he reminded us several times that it was not a service. Afterwards, we all complimented him on a fine and touching non-service...(*Out of Iowa*, p. 120)

Focus on key words that are out of place today-- rich tidbits worthy of elaboration. Why *manure*? Fertilizer hadn't been invented yet. What else was unique about farming back then? What are the implications around the lack of penicillin? *Gangrene*. Now there's a tidbit for you. So is *polio*. *Strep infections* left many a child with permanent heart damage. What about three *babies dying*? How does that happen? No incubators yet, and when introduced, too much oxygen was used and *babies were blinded*. Children died from an *overdose of anesthesia* while having tonsils removed. A family could lose two or more children in a matter of weeks to *measles*. The *Civil War* affected every family.

You can bet some of these tidbits are prominent in your family's history. Bring the subjects up to people in interviews. Mine them. They are biographical gold.

Not all tidbits are historical. When writing a biography include tidbits about the person's life today. Bring the reader up to date. The present is important. It reflects from where the person came, and soon it will be part of their history. In writing your memoir, you could say simply: "Now in my sixties, every morning when I awake I am grateful for another day of independence." Or, you could mine it and say:

Every morning when I awake, before I put my feet on the fluffy rug beside my bed, I'm grateful for another day of independence. I mention the fluffy rug because I'm into feel good things these days. High heels and tight jeans have gone by the wayside. In stores I feel fabrics to make certain they pass the feel good test before even taking an item off the rack. My jammies are soft, the bedding high-thread-count Egyptian cotton, the towels fluffy, and my sofa has been reupholstered in a fabric that feels like flannel.

When you are in your sixties, discomfort for the sake of appearances or propriety falls by the wayside. You begin to take steps to soften your world and that of others. You find yourself into comfort food..."

You have just transitioned to another topic where you elaborate on meatloaf and lemon cake, and then perhaps you transition to another comfort, the morning ceremony of drinking coffee with snow falling outside and you are no longer concerned about the traffic report.

Everyday experiences are tidbits worth mining. Whether they are in the person's past or present, they are part of a life story and worthy of beautifully descriptive words that paint the person's universe. How people exist in the world determines their role in it. A person living in the context of gratefulness is important to write about--a vital lesson for others. Life is not all about spellbinding experiences. Trivial events are fascinating. This is why it is inaccurate to assume a life is not interesting.

Expressive words describe what being in your sixties, seventies, or eighties is like, which is quite different and surprisingly sunnier than young readers expect. Through descriptive detail, you give them a rare and precious gift by modeling the aging process through a fresh and buoyant perspective. If an objective for writing your life story is to inspire a younger generation, this will do it by countering pre-conceived notions and introducing a new model for aging.

This does not mean you put a rosy spin on everything. Don't avoid unpleasant topics. It is possible to write about personal losses by demonstrating stalwart strength and perseverance

carried the message from them throughout life. In his mind, the expression conveyed in a hook is a universal truth, and maybe it is.

Another way to discover defining moments is to ask interviewees if they could live one experience in their life over again, excluding the obvious ones of marriage and birth of babies, what would it be.

> Uncle Bob, with a sly grin and a twinkle in his eye, answered this question with: "I can't tell you." That said a lot, and the response alone is worth including in his life story. It was so him. I didn't stop there, though, and soon he was talking about hunting wildcats in Oregon and getting paid to do it.

Discover defining moments and capture the back story. Once you do that, you will know: **You can write.**

Technique 5
EXPOSE REBEL JEWELS

Everyone has incidents in their history where they broke away from the mainstream and did the unconventional. The result might be glory days or miserable consequences. Often people are ashamed of devastating failures, but those failures are powerful biographical jewels replete with lessons learned and evidence of amazing growth. Human frailty and the struggle to overcome adversity draws readers in. Conversely, enthralling details of blazing triumphs are heartwarming. Either way, your audience will relate on some level.

Whether it is your life or someone else's you are writing about, be brave. Take a peek at bold departures, hurts, resentments, betrayals, and unfortunate choices. Convey the pain they reveal, the festering wounds they left behind, and the lingering heartaches. Examine the scars.

My man left, and I was devastated. At my regular nail appointment I shared what happened with my manicurist. I cried and she cried. Soon the other manicurists around us and their customers became intrigued by the emotional turmoil and got in on the story and the misery, and they cried. I mean, it was a sad, sad, sorrowful situation.

Hairdressers became curious about all the drama and teary emotion, and they and their customers were soon swept into the doom and gloom. Every woman in there knew in her soul it could happen to her, and a dark, angry cloud came down and swallowed us all up as though the life force was being sucked out of us. As we sank deeper and deeper into the abyss, our only defense was bashing...which further ravaged the anguished group. The cloud darkened, the gloom deepened, and happy salon chatter turned into melancholy whispers and awkward silence. It was grim.

Later, sitting in my car as I was leaving, I glanced back inside the shop. A lady had just entered and was looking around like: "What happened?" It was blatantly clear that in spite of all the pretty hair and fingernails, I had single handedly brought this normally cheerful, chatty, upbeat place down, down, down into the depths of despair. I mean, Dante could not have done it better.

Given the nature of the betrayal, I should have been
thinking: "You aren't leaving, thank god, are you?" Instead,
I was feeling like the victim of a drive-by shooting, and I
shared that with everybody. I should have brought
champagne and cake, but I brought Dante. Realizing this
was a defining moment, and it changed everything. Going
forward, I still wrestled with the in-your-face demons of the
loss, but I determined then and there that I was going to save
myself from the doom and gloom.

I couldn't do it, though. In spite of all that resolve, I just
could not pull it off. The wound was too deep, the pain
unrelenting, and the scar everlasting, and that was the end of
love as I knew it...(*Out of Iowa*, pp. 247, 248)

Once you have laid the emotions bare, describe
the resilience that fortified the person to rise
again and continue on. It is possible to mine
rebel jewels without trashing the subject or
anyone else involved by staying connected with
emotions rather than bad behaviors. Whether
actions are justified or not, emotions always
resonate with others. By focusing on them, you
can produce a penetrating and touching story
demonstrating that: **You can write.**

*(See more examples of these five techniques in
the Appendix.)*

These five techniques will get you started
writing, and more writing tips are forthcoming as
we consider the subsequent developmental stages
of creating a biography. You will learn how to
take the short stories you wrote and string them

together in a logical pattern with flow and continuity.

Before doing that, however, it is important to understand the purpose of the first draft. While writing it, focus on uninhibited regurgitation of memories and emotions. Use the five techniques presented above during the first draft process only if they don't get in the way. If they do, apply them later. There will be plenty of opportunities to do so. For now, be a wild, reckless, unchecked scribe.

THE FIRST DRAFT: The objective of the first draft is to resurrect as many memories as possible as well as the feelings accompanying them. Start writing by getting these memories and feelings out of your head and down on paper or into a computer. Don't censor yourself. Write anything you want any way it comes out--let the thoughts flow. Write with abandon.

Don't worrying about the quality of your writing while producing the first draft. Just write whatever comes into your head, not necessarily in any logical order or in a comprehensive manner. **You have a license in the first draft stage to do some really inferior, sloppy, randomly incoherent writing.**

In fact, for the first draft you can forget much of what I've said so far. Forget about the audience, ignore the goals and objectives, abandon your sensitivities, and don't focus on technique. For this initial stage, it is all about you and your visceral self. Enjoy.

> Write for yourself and no one else, especially if you are writing your own biography. Consider facts, details, and feelings, but don't be constrained by them. Be self-indulgent. Introduce your accomplishments. Describe your witty nature and sparkling personality and charm but also be candid about faults, miscalculations, unfortunate choices, and limitations. Cultivate introspection and self-awareness--be raw.

Later you will create a working copy from this first draft and shift your frame of reference to that of the audience. With wave after wave you will embellish and refine that working draft, apply the five techniques, and shape it for sharing with others. For now, though, this first draft is yours and yours alone. No one needs to see it but you. Vent.

When you start writing, memories are triggered as you go through the day. You think you will remember them later, but no matter how many memory enhancing drugs you take or crossword puzzles you work to exercise the brain, when you sit down to write, you won't be able to recall many of them.

79

HINT: Carry a pen and paper at all times and jot down notes. Put a small hand-held recorder in your purse or car or leave messages on your phone. Don't forget those riveting thoughts that pop into your head. You want all of them in your comprehensive first draft.

When the first draft is finished, print a hard copy and store it in a safe place. Copy the computerized file to a working file and save the original file as a permanent record. As you develop your book, much of what you wrote in the first draft will not be used, but you don't want to lose it. Preserve it. **A universal rule for writers is: Always keep everything you write.**

After months of writing the first draft have drained your brain, you are ready to move on to a working draft in which you craft a story suitable for sharing with others. Before you do, though, there is something you should ponder because it will influence what you take with you from that first draft to the book you will eventually share. It has to do with *frame of reference*--the core from which you write.

FRAME OF REFERENCE: In the first draft, you wrote for yourself. Now you are going to write for others. To do this well, you need to think about some things. What do you want to accomplish with your book? Who is your audience, and what impact do you want to have on them? What do you want readers to experience when they read it? Knowing the answers to these questions will facilitate your writing.

> I imagined a devoted elderly aunt's face lighting up when she read my story. She invested so much in me; I wanted her to see the return. I thought about my grandkids reading it as teenagers and perhaps thinking Grandma was way cooler than they imagined. I wanted the next generation of nieces, nephews, and cousins to understand the legacy of my parents and to appreciate family connections. I sought to poke fun at my flaws and idiot behavior while being shamelessly egocentric about recording hard-earned accomplishments. I wanted to share wisdom and lessons learned, hoping to soften the fall or inspire the climb of descendants and other young people as they shape their own lives. I aspired to re-define aging by sharing my voyage through productive and fulfilling "encore years."

That's a lot. Maybe you don't have an audience and you are doing this just for yourself. That's fine, too. An introspective life review produces fresh, mature perspectives which are healing. Whatever your motives, set up a mental framework around why you are chronicling your life or someone else's and what you hope to accomplish by doing so.

As you move into the working file stage in which you produce a life story to share with others, keep this frame of reference in mind. Serving as a compass, it is your guide to what to take out, what to leave in, and how to say it.

WORKING DRAFT: Once that sloppy, outrageous, and inevitably embarrassing first draft is finished, when you've had enough introspection, self-indulgence, victim mentality, guilt, and shameless bliss to last a lifetime, copy it to a working file and begin an endless parade of draft revisions. The fun begins--the creation, the art, the polish, and the birth of a life story.

TABLE OF CONTENTS: Create a *table of contents*. It helps identify chapters and facilitates developing a cohesive, global vision of the book. Chapters, topics, and paragraphs move around as the story takes shape so the *table* must remain fluid, but it provides a framework to organize incremental story-by-story accounts into a logical sequence so the book flows. Choose words in the *table of contents* thoughtfully. Potential buyers refer to it when making purchasing decisions. It is important.

OUTTAKES: Assuring good flow requires moving things around, adding to them, and sometimes taking them out entirely. Set up an "outtakes file." Transfer into it from the working draft anything you don't want to include in the final book. Don't throw writing away. You will be surprised how often you bring outtakes back into the working draft or at least refer to them.

When going through the first working draft of regurgitated information copied from the first draft and deciding what to keep and what to take out, consider generational insight. What is ordinary and uninteresting to you might be quite a novelty to your children or grandchildren, especially if you describe it in colorful detail.

For example, the fears, emotions, turmoil, intrusion, and disruption families experienced as a result of the military draft might seem ordinary to those of us who experienced it, but subsequent generations will have no sense of the impact on families unless someone depicts that for them. Future generations may never gather eggs, drive a standard shift, mechanic a car, sew anything, take an appliance in for repair, gather around a radio, listen in on a party line, or watch a black and white television show with the screen rolling.

INTRODUCTION: Here is where you tell why you wrote the book and why someone should read it. You also disclose interesting things about the process of writing it, include qualifiers and disclaimers, describe the scope of the life story, and set the stage for the real chapters to come. If you change names or details of events in the book, disclose that here. **Don't begin the story in the introduction. You are setting the stage, not writing the story.**

> **HINT: Go to a library or book store and review introductions in biographical books to get a flavor of what to include. You will see examples of what to do and what not to do.**

Studies show that few people read introductions. When looking at the excessively long paragraphs in many of them, it is easy to understand why. Break up paragraphs. Add indentations and white space. Be creative. Introductions can be boring. Don't be afraid to use humor as I did in the introduction to my biography:

Today at sixty-something I have a vibrant, purposeful plan for my next thirty years. Although at times I feel that the older I get, the better I was, in reality I am more vigorous than ever. Life has never been better. That is, except for the people living in my attic who sneak down at night to steal slippers, hide reading glasses, and disable the TV remote. (*Out of Iowa*, p. 14)

It is a good idea in a biography introduction to include a statement about "the truth." Explain that everyone's perception of it is different, that memories are selective, and that people create their own stories in their minds about things that happened. Additionally, over time memories fade, and when people recall events, they reconstruct them. Your story is yours as you see it. Others may see it differently. Suggesting in the introduction that everyone filters events through their own reality and acknowledging the fact that there are divergent interpretations of the past show respect for the views of others while defending your own.

ORGANIZATION: The key to the good overall flow of a book is organization. After stringing stories together and organizing them within the framework of the *table of contents*, bring balance to the random writings. Arrange them so that the humorous, high-intensity, and more mundane but critical parts are interspersed throughout. If a chapter is weak, rework it.

Structure the book so it has a beginning, middle and end. Grab the audience with the beginning and wow them with something meaningful at the end that pulls everything together, summing up the major theme. Fill the middle with references to the beginning and to earlier chapters. Build to the end.

There is a propensity to present information chronologically in a biography. That makes sense to some extent, but if this approach is done exclusively the book tends to read like a diary, journal, or genealogy report.

Selecting chapters by topics such as people, location, event, or some other category and running those over whatever timeline applies to them are more interesting. For example, write a chapter on grandparents, or Montana, or parenting, or the high school years. Perhaps you have a whole chapter on a significant event, a family crisis, romance, career, a hobby, or a beloved pet.

THE FIRST PARAGRAPH: Determine the most important message in the book and get that in the first paragraph. Do it in a way that captivates the reader. Think of a publisher looking at the book and reading only the first paragraph or two. Would he be interested enough to keep reading? Would someone picking up the book in an airport gift shop or a book store be motivated to buy it after reading the first few sentences? Nail the first paragraph.

HINT: For an example of this, read the first couple of paragraphs in *Water for Elephants*, by Sara Gruen. It will draw you in. You may not be inclined to read a book about circuses, but that first

paragraph will suck you in and change your mind. You will be captivated.

Just as the first few paragraphs of the first chapter should grab the reader and tell what the book is about, the first few paragraphs of every chapter should do the same.

THE THEME: Everyone's life has several themes. They emerge from the first draft. A theme is a person's way of being in the world, a frame of reference that runs throughout his life and drives behaviors and choices. The introspective nature of biographical writing is a perfect opportunity to identify and understand themes in your life and those of your parents, siblings, and others. As you forage through the past, these themes are revealed, and they resonate as dramatic influences.

When you identify the predominant theme of a life and refer to it throughout the book, a common thread is woven from beginning to end. Mention it in the introduction to set the stage, refer to it throughout, and nail it in the last chapter. The theme might be craving excitement and taking risks. It may be behavior common to a slow and steady nature or a creative, artsy one. To some people it's all about money and achievement, and to others it is about animals. Some people collect things and others collect people. A theme reflects how a person interacts with the world. It defines him.

I discovered the theme of "rescue" as I developed my biography, and it explained a lot. I was a passionate rescuer. Themes of "having something to prove" and "just trying to matter" also surfaced. I ran all of these throughout the biography. It was revealing how rescuing, having something to prove, and trying to matter coalesced into a powerful force for achievement and a persistent quest for proactive solutions to problems. Rescue.

FINDING YOUR STYLE: Once the basic organization is established, edit the working draft. Refine the copy using the *five writing techniques*. Writing a biography is not creating an academic document. Write like you talk. At the suggestion of a writing class instructor, I took contractions out of my biography draft because that is supposedly more proper. Later I regretted having done so because it didn't sound like me, so I put many of them back.

If this is your first serious writing effort, it may take awhile to find your style, but as you progress, a certain way of saying things will become comfortable for you. Have the courage to be unique, expressive, quirky, and true to yourself. Be proper or unconventional, whichever suits you.

I took a novel approach to creating the index in *Out of Iowa*. I naturally posed questions when writing the book, so the index consists of a list of questions with the associated page numbers. From these questions you can pretty much find your way around the book.

I also included in the last chapter a bulleted list of over a hundred lessons learned from my life experiences, many of which were illustrated in the biographical story itself. I inserted humor throughout this list to overcome the increasingly short attention spans of young people who are accustomed to multi-tasking and obtaining short bursts of information from a cell phone.

You can stray from common practices, but in the final product, don't deviate from basic grammar, punctuation, and sentence construction requirements. Seek an editor and produce a professional, polished biography worthy of the person it is portraying.

That said, let me introduce some contradictions. First, it is better to do some things half way than not at all. Writing a biography is one of those things. Secondly, grammarians argue ardently over all kinds of grammatical and punctuation rules, so getting all that right is as exercise in futility. Don't get all in a wad over being perfect. We are not writing a thesis here. The goal is to communicate, not to get an A. Thirdly, your natural writing style might be so quirky and irreverent that you can get by with almost anything. The epitome of unsophistication can be zany and goofball enough to generate buzz and make everyone want to read the book. Writing playfully so you don't appear so alarmingly off that someone schedules an intervention or outlines a treatment plan, you could be wildly successful by avoiding the norm and following eccentric instincts. If being boring is your biggest fear, go ahead and turn your crazy, mad, flamboyant self loose. (Send me a copy.)

THE STORY: There are only 26 letters in the alphabet, and from them I wrote an 90,000 word memoir. Amazing. Ah, the magic of language and the written word. Milk this magic for all it is worth. Turn the working draft into a story.

Begin polishing, enhancing, and arranging the text in the working file. Then print what you've written in hard copy. Working from it, re-consider chapter and story sequence. Move things around to logical sub-headings while focusing on flow and balance. This is much easier to do from hard copy than from a computer screen. Firm up the *table of contents*.

HINT: You are going to need hard copies periodically throughout the book

development process. **Printing a book draft on a home printer is expensive (paper, ink, wear and tear), and it is time consuming. A better option is to electronically place print orders with companies like Kinkos where you get same day delivery. Place orders online at** *printonline.kinkos.com,* **upload the file, and go to Kinko's a few hours later to pick it up, or take a flash drive into the store. Have the file printed on both sides of the paper and designate black and white printing to keep costs down. A 200 page manuscript will cost about $20.**

If same day delivery is not required, an online *print on demand* **(POD) company may be the best option. Many can deliver a softback, bound proof in three to four days. I get proofs for about $5 each from Create Space, a company owned by Amazon, (details in** *Chapter 8 - Printing).*

Check facts and verify as much information as possible with others. Qualify memories you are not sure of by stating that this is how you remember it. Perhaps you insert other people's interpretations when they are different from your own. That can be interesting.

Use feelings, thoughts, and your inferences generously while being aware that they may not be someone else's truth. Anticipate the perceptions of others and consider the validity of your memories and theirs. Write a story that is mindful and respectful of other memories, but don't disregard or sacrifice your perspective. Bottom line, if someone sees things differently, they can write their own book.

PROFOUND MESSAGES: Scripting a story is a rare opportunity to convey meaningful messages to young people. Seek out significant lessons emanating from the lives of others. Emphasize sacrifices and demonstrate how people before them invested in the future of those who follow. Strive to elicit pride among readers who discover for the first time details of their predecessors' experiences. Where appropriate, present the subjects of the biography as role models--indomitable sources of inspiration and encouragement. Don't miss this uncommon occasion to be instrumental in using profound messages to spark a sense of heritage and to suggest a worthy path.

HISTORICAL CONNECTIONS: Look for ways to intersect life's events with historical ones. Portraying the context of a person's experiences this way is a history lesson for generations to come. Explore feelings about historical events. **It was not the cold war itself that was significant about my generation's childhood. It was the fear it provoked.**

I compared my generation's cold war fears (fallout shelters, scary training films on nuclear blasts, and potential annihilation by the Russians) to the fear of terrorism today. This was a revelation to my children who had no concept of that challenging time. Every generation has its historical nightmares, wars, and tribulations that provide intriguing story opportunities. The impact of Vietnam on my family was profound while to my children it is a vague historical reference. My dad experienced the gnawing apprehension of the draft during World War II, and my four brothers did the same a generation later. History takes on meaning when portrayed in the context of consequences to one's family.

CHARACTER DEVELOPMENT: Develop people into the interesting, complex, vulnerable characters they are. Describe them in detail both from a physical and personality perspective. Make them sympathetic characters so readers relate. Concentrate on the essence of the person.

Perhaps you describe Uncle Hank as Noah-like and sturdy, or Aunt Edith as fragile and waif-ish, or a couch potato as someone tending toward inertia, and then expand on those descriptions. A brother is portrayed as simply ornery, or you elaborate and call him intentionally playful and unintentionally a bully. Describe someone who always wears black as suddenly looking like a piñata when they show up in color. Search a thesaurus for just the right words to uniquely characterize each person.

> **HINT: A thesaurus can be your best friend. If you struggle with describing someone or something, plug a word close to that description into an online thesaurus and find a better one. Try not to use the same word twice in a paragraph. A reviewer once complimented me on my vocabulary. It was the thesaurus.**

I was told in a seminar that technically if you are using real people in a book you should have written permission unless you change their names, descriptions, and backgrounds so they are not easily recognizable. I didn't do that. After perusing biographies in book stores and libraries, I got a sense that other writers don't do it either. (In most states, there is no cause of action for slander if a person is dead.) At any rate, by developing characters in as flattering a light as possible without substantially misrepresenting anything, I felt comfortable with including people without asking them to sign a release.

Sticking to facts and being as accurate and truthful as possible, making touchy topics entertaining or heartwarming, and omitting the ugly stuff reduces the likelihood that someone will take issue with what you write. Cranky old Aunt Hazel might get a kick out of your description of her and the outrageous stories about her if you paint her in the right light. She is probably innately proud of her contrary disposition. Label her spunky instead of grumpy and zany instead of really, really weird.

> **HINT: In the case of truly unsympathetic characters whom you don't want to leave out, say something nice about them followed by a comment such as: "But, in all other ways she was not someone you'd ask to dinner. The problem, of course, was that you had to eat dinner with her every night." You make your point without creating legal fodder.**

If you have concerns about including a living person in your story without their written approval and you don't want to leave them out, contact an attorney.

I chose not to let legal fears complicate the process of telling my life story or keep me from realizing my writing dreams. If something legal comes up, I'll deal with it. I suspect that is a remote possibility. Perhaps we get more courageous about such things as we get older. When you are ninety-something and run out of money or are the last man standing, you can be an outrageous rebel and write anything you want--a reason to keep that first draft. There is a perverse synergy to that, and perhaps it is something to boost the spirit when contemplating living that long. Ain't life grand?

BIASES: With the uninhibited first draft where memories flow freely onto paper, biases and opinions are reflected in the content. These are valid as our interpretations of life, but just because we think something in our head doesn't make it universally true. Others have their own thoughts and their own personal truth. Avoid being too preachy. Consider removing or softening biases. It's okay to have opinions, but you are not writing this book to sway people to your beliefs, but rather to capture a life story.

It is challenging to accomplish the objective of sharing wisdom with future generations without coming across as preachy. Since conveying lessons learned may be one of the major reasons you write your story and because your beliefs are an integral part of you, go ahead and include a few opinions and philosophical meanderings in the final manuscript. Work to soften them with humor and express an appreciation for the divergent opinions of others to take the edge off and to show respect for those you are trying to reach with your messages. Don't let opinions overwhelm your biography. If you want to write a manifesto, do so, but that is not a life story.

RUN-THROUGHS: This is a laborious but exhilarating re-writing process. It is where the magic happens. A valuable tool for the novice writer who thinks he cannot write, this process involves going over a working draft many times, each time with a different objective--building the story in layers. Every run-through layers another level of depth and polish onto the manuscript.

With every pass you will still be building, enhancing, rounding out, embellishing, and re-organizing the story as well as improving the quality of the mechanics (format, punctuation, grammar, and spelling). However, the primary objective of each pass will have a specific objective. This gives every run-through a purpose. By focusing on a specific objective throughout each pass, the book becomes increasingly robust, more cohesive and the flow improves. **If you are not a writer, run-throughs will make you one.**

In addition to the *five techniques* which you apply throughout the writing process, here are things to focus on during run-throughs. Some passes go quickly and others are tedious and take a huge investment of time. All are worthwhile.

RUN-THROUGH OBJECTIVES

- **Develop characters:** backgrounds, physical descriptions, speech, perspectives, temperaments, ways of being in the world, quirks, character, talents, flaws, vulnerabilities, strengths, how the person dresses and moves, how they express themselves, and how they influence others.

- **Add descriptive detail:** Develop scenes, describe settings, cultures, environments, smells, colors, textures, structures, noises, temperatures, and terrain.

- **Add dialogue and quotes:** Sprinkle them throughout the manuscript. Portray how people express themselves.

- **Relate personal experiences to historical events:** Paint a picture of unique historical happenings--the big bang events of the time or a minor thing with major consequences. Describe the time and place in which the person lived.

- **Make minor things major:** Build them out. Explore colorful, descriptive ways to paint a picture and add meaning. Target things that no longer exist and that are foreign to young people. Contrast them with today's world.

- **Organize the stories:** Print a hard copy of the draft and rearrange the stories. Massage the table of contents.

- **Use sentiment:** Describe feelings, spiritual connections, passions, and relationships with people, animals, nature, and the world while removing unnecessary self-indulgent remarks.

- **Interject humor:** Consider the light side of stories. Keep jokes going by referring to them throughout a chapter or the entire book.

- **Tighten up:** Don't state the obvious. Remove unnecessary words and redundant sentences and paragraphs.

- **Incorporate a theme throughout:** Introduce it in the first chapter, build it in throughout (don't overdo it), and zap it in the ending.

- **Create transitions:** Assure a flow from sentence to sentence, paragraph to paragraph and chapter to chapter.

- **Write in an active voice**: Probably the most profound thing an author can do to improve his writing is to write in an active voice as opposed to a passive voice. (Google: *grammar/active vs passive voice*)

- **Enhance writing technique:** Take out as many "I's," "me's," "my's," "you's," and "your's" as possible without jeopardizing the story. Eliminate has, had, and have where you can. Use "would" and "could" only for situations involving uncertainty.

Writers have a tendency to overuse "it," "some," "any," "can" and "all." Eliminate them where possible. In the case of "it," consider substituting a more descriptive word. In some cases, you should completely rewrite to avoid using these words. They are okay to use, but do so judiciously and appropriately. Use "that," "which," and "who" correctly.

- **Eliminate distracting words:** Don't use unnecessary or redundant adjectives or adverbs. If a word ends in "ly," consider taking it out. Use words like "very," "really," "rather," and "pretty" sparingly. Rarely are they necessary and they can be trite. Evaluate the value of every word.

- **Enhance and improve:** Go over every sentence and improve it, then reconsider the order of the sentences in a paragraph. In general, put the strongest sentences at the beginning or end of a paragraph. Use variations in sentence structures.

- **Look for words or phrases to emphasize:** Italicize, put things in quotes, or bold them for emphasis. Don't overdo it. Bolding and quotation marks can be particularly distracting. Be economical with their use.

- **Enhance format:** Introduce white space. Break up long paragraphs, indent whole paragraphs for emphasis, use bullets and create lists. (Don't use tabs to indent. Use spaces. This is a formatting requirement for electronic books, and it is becoming standard.) Set off dialogue.

- **Enhance word selection:** Use more interesting, colorful, and descriptive words. Put words into an online thesaurus and find better ones. If you used a word twice in a paragraph, find another one. If you can't think of the perfect word, put a less than perfect one in the thesaurus and see what comes up.

- **Deepen descriptions:** Embellish and describe something by comparing it to something else. Add descriptive detail that paints a picture. Use metaphors and similes. Don't overdo.

- **Repeat elements:** In *Out of Iowa* I used tools to relate completely separate events to each other: Dad's tools used to charcoal, Mom's tools opened a bottle of wine, and Grandma used a tot's toy tools to get him to eat macaroni.

- **Check the organization:** Print a hard copy and review it for good flow and rhythm. Make certain that sequences make sense. Look for a beginning, middle, and ending in the book as a whole and within each chapter.

- **Check spelling:** Read word by word and syllable by syllable. Verify spelling of any questionable words.

- **Check punctuation:** Obtain an authoritative source book and use it to assure consistent application of punctuation rules.

- **Check grammar:** Review for subject and verb agreement, proper tense usage, sentence structure, etc.

- **Read the manuscript fresh:** Let it bake. Put it aside for a week or so and then do another run-through.

- **Read the manuscript out loud:** This will reveal awkward sentence structure. The words should flow smoothly. Seek rhythm while assuring variation of sentence structure. Improve transitions from word to word, paragraph to paragraph, and chapter to chapter.

- **Read the manuscript from a hard copy.** Search for errors.

- **Read the manuscript wearing other hats:** Pretend you are other people. View stories from their perspectives. Seek perspectives that show more sides of the story.

- **Read the manuscript from the perspective of your harshest critic:** Polish it so it is difficult for him to effectively challenge anything in it.

- **Read the manuscript for fun:** Did the tone and content reflect--your vision and purpose? Did you enjoy it?

- **Repeat all of the above.**

These run-throughs might be daunting, but going over and over the manuscript is how writing is done. You will be rereading and reworking it many times anyway, and this gives each iteration a purpose. I went through my biography, my first writing effort, over sixty times in the period of a year. That is why it takes so long to write a book. If you could just knock it out, read it through a few times and publish a great book, you would be a masterful writing genius. Most of us are not that. In fact, no writer does that.

Think of it as massaging the book, enhancing it, and giving it life. Relish and enjoy the creative aspect of the run-throughs. Remarkable progress is made with each one. You will marvel at how much better the most recent draft is from the previous one, so much so that it becomes difficult to end the process and go to print. You have learned that one more run-through will yield a substantially enhanced manuscript.

EFFICIENT WRITING: After the first few drafts, begin writing "tightly" with minimum words, no repetitive thoughts, and no sentences or paragraphs that say the same thing only differently. Use words that end in "ly" sparsely and don't use two or more adverbs or adjectives together that mean the same thing. The greatest comment I got on a business book I wrote was: "There was not a wasted word in it." Go through drafts periodically and remove unnecessary words, sentences, and even paragraphs. Be brutal. Make every word count.

WRITE STRONG: Make every sentence meaningful--each one communicating something interesting, entertaining, or emotionally compelling; conveying a lesson learned; or providing information that contributes to the story. Use qualifiers (very, really, rather, pretty) sparingly. A sentence is stronger without them.

> **HINT: Use the "find" capability on the text software to efficiently target words throughout the text for possible deletion or replacement. (This "find" capability can be your best friend--a vital tool for efficiently enhancing a document.)**

Write in the active voice. (Google: *grammar/ active vs passive voice* to learn how to do this.) Take the words "can," "would," "have," "had," "was," "been," "be," and "will" out where possible and rewrite using powerful verbs. Don't say "I have done" something. Say you did it. Don't say Dad "would" start the fire or a fire was started by Dad. Say he started it.

TRANSITIONS: Once you have done enough run-throughs that the order of things is fairly set and the *table of contents* established, focus on the transition run-through. Develop solid transitions from one sentence to another, one paragraph to another, and one chapter to another. Having a good *flow* to a book is vital to readability and keeping the reader's attention.

> **HINT: Portions of the text that don't flow well or are awkward are revealed when reading the text out loud and from a hard copy. (Sometimes, though, an intentional abrupt shift can create a dramatic effect.)**

At the end of each chapter, entice the reader to continue on to the next one so he doesn't put the book down. This is done by ending the chapter with a question, a cliff hanger, or teasing the reader with hints about what is to come.

Once you've developed a character, refer to him in subsequent pages of the book. Romance and relationships are compelling topics and prime candidates for echoing throughout a book. Gripping story lines, themes, and transitions make a book a page-turner.

HUMOR AND EMOTION: Include something for everyone (every age group) in the biography and interject humor or emotion throughout. Bring a smile to the readers face or, conversely, a tear to his eye, or give him such a strong lesson that it touches him in a profound way. Nothing lifts the spirit like humor, and you can make just about anything humorous.

Technology is not a very funny subject. It can even be annoying. Such annoying topics, done lightheartedly and without being overtly grumpy, are entertaining.

Love Me Some Technology
Excerpts from *Out of Iowa*

I embrace technology because I have to, not because I want to, and I will take whatever medication is required to make that happen...

I watched my two-year-old granddaughter proficiently and intently navigating a multitude of apps on an iPhone in a restaurant and realized the toys stashed in my purse held little interest for her. The most amazing thing, though, is that it is clear I'll never catch up to where she is today, and she is two! In spite of the fact that anything electronic makes me feel like a cat scratching on linoleum, I must enter the world of technology. I do so kicking and screaming, with grave trepidation, and a peculiar sense of adventure...

...a young technical genius was demonstrating features on my new laptop and asked me to select a song to download...I couldn't think of any (a senior moment), so he suggested Simon and Garfunkel. I told him I was way cooler than that and requested a Snoop Dog number. I really don't know much about Snoop Dog, except that he must be hip since he goes around with his pants on the ground and that we have a common interest in gardening. I know this because he raps about garden tools, you know, hoes, and he has a fascination with grass...Anyway, I made my point. We settled on Jimmy Buffet...

...the Apple store children have a special appeal because nowhere else do young people engage my generation unless they need a co-signer or a low-mileage car. Although young folks are generally a challenge to captivate, it is important that we maintain a connection with them. They may not realize it, but they need us for our wisdom, and we need them to put Rod Stewart ringtones on our phones and Grand Canyon screen savers on our computers. When I accidentally take a picture of my feet with my iPhone, they can show me how to get it on Facebook...(*Out of Iowa*, pp. 233-236)

Conveying humor in everyday events and revealing the emotions behind behavior or words make a book entertaining and personal. These are the qualities that stimulate memories, touch people, make them laugh or cry, or inspire them to deliver May Baskets to your front porch.

HOOKS: Become a master at identifying hooks. Hooks are crisp, colorful, snappy sayings that are easy to recall--short sentences or phrases that carry a big wallop because they are efficient and meaningful to the person saying them. They reflect a person's view of the world. For example: If someone frequently says, "Nothing good happens after midnight," you know there are experiences behind that statement.

Comments that people frequently make are strong indications of what they are about. Everyone has emphatic beliefs. They are anthems, kind of. A crazy friend of mine often says: "I have issues," and she does. Another says: "It's raining men, hallelujah!" I don't think it is raining men now that disco is "out" and my thirties are behind me, but clearly she does. Good for her. An old fellow in my hometown was always saying: "Don't affect me none." It was like his theme song, and it defined him. You have to wonder what experiences he had that made him say that--to shut himself off like that.

Hooks can reflect vulnerabilities and fortitude or joys and bold confidence. Seek out the hooks that reflect your view of the world. When interviewing others, do the same. Then explore the life experiences that generated them and the consequences they provoke.

CRITIQUES: When the manuscript is in its latter stages, run it by others. It is a generous act for a person to read a draft and provide feedback. (Acknowledge them in the book.) Some will never get around to reading it. Most will be encouraging, perhaps too much so. If they are friends or relatives, they are going to love, love, love what you wrote.

Ask them to be brutal. Your having a bad day over candid criticism is a small sacrifice to make for a better book. To encourage meaningful input, ask specific questions like:

What did you like best?

Where can I improve the book?
Is anything inaccurate?
Were you confused by anything?
What needs more development?
What was the weakest chapter?

When people give input, don't respond by justifying your position. Accept the advice, thank them, and adopt the suggestions you deem appropriate. People may give bad advice. By studying writing, you may know more than your reviewers. Whether this is true or not, as the author, you have the final say. It's your book. Use prudent judgement when accepting advice.

If you thought writing a book was a simple process, this chapter has probably changed your mind. Still, through writing life stories, you discover a fascinating pastime. If you commit to the processes presented herein, you will prove that: **You can write.**

Through that writing, you articulated how the unique, fascinating life you wrote about mattered--more than anyone knew. You attached meaning to the life by celebrating it with words, conveying the essence of a person that otherwise would not have been explored or revealed. Because you did this, your life matters more. You made your mark; you created a legacy, and you were relevant. Productive, determined, and passionate enough to create for others an enduring treasure that honors a person through demonstrating their relevance, you captured life. Everyone just wants to matter. Writers matter.

Next you must transform what you wrote into a tangible object, an entirely different process from writing. Producing a book requires cautious strategy and informed decision making. It makes the book real, and, in spite of the challenges, you are going to have some fun now.

- II -

THE MECHANICS
OF CREATING
A BIOGRAPHY

**You are never going to have the perfect book.
The important thing is that you have one.**

Chapter -5-

WRITING MECHANICS

There is a material functional difference between writing a book and producing it. Surrounding the creative writing process are the mechanics of presenting it in a professional, polished way. If not done well, these things distract readers. Unfortunately, the mechanics are tedious, but it is important to do them well so the story and its heartwarming messages shine through.

FORMATTING: This involves designing the presentation of the document and requires mastering a substantial amount of detail. Learning how to format the text of a book is a bit intimidating if you've never done it before, but proficiency produces a valuable skill with many cross applications. Let's get started.

Book Size: Part of formatting is deciding on the outer measurements of the book. This will affect the page setup. There are standard sizes. If you vary from them, it may cost more to print, and it can narrow your printer vendor choices. Most printers have their own standard sizes, but *5 1/2* *x 8 1/2* and *6 x 9* are fairly universal. I used 6 x 9 for all my books, a popular size.

If you are not going to publish and sell the biography and you just plan to produce a few copies for family and friends, consider the standard page size of 8 1/2 x 11. This is discussed in detail in *Chapter 8 - Printing*.

Font: This involves the size of the letters and the style of type. *Letter size* of text typically runs from 9 to 14 points, depending on how friendly you want the readability to be for your audience. The letter size also affects the number of pages and the thickness of the book. The size for my biography, *Out of Iowa,* is 11 points. I used 13 here. I wanted to be friendly.

> **HINT: The computer screen does not always accurately represent the print size as it will appear on hard copy. Print a few pages early on to determine if you are satisfied with the letter size.**

When selecting the *style of type*, use one of the more common ones. Exotic styles are distracting. Styles that have a little curl (serif) on certain letters like the "r" "y" and "a" are more friendly because people are conditioned to them. This book is in "Times New Roman" (some curls). My biography is in "Georgia" (lots of curls), a traditional type. "Arial" is a common type if you want a more modern, sleek style. It has no curl factor and reads easily on a screen. Like the font size, the style of type can affect the number of pages and the thickness of the book.

HINT: When selecting a type style, check out how the italics show up. In some, the distinction between regular type and italics is so minor that italics don't stand out adequately, which is one of the main reasons you use them.

Spacing: It is possible to make the text easier on the eye by setting the spacing between letters wider. Standard spacing between characters is set at 0. This document is set at 5.

HINT: Historically, the custom was to put two spaces after a period at the end of a sentence. The current trend is to use one space, which I have done here.

You can also adjust spacing between lines. I don't recommend that for text, but it might be appropriate for wording on the cover. The standard is "1" which is what I used here.

Avoid "widows" (single lines at the beginning or end of a page), single words at the end of a paragraph, and "rivers" (spaces trailing down through the text of a paragraph). Don't indent by using the "tab" on the keyboard. It creates problems for the printer.

White space: The more white space on the page, the friendlier the text. Break the text up by indenting whole paragraphs, avoiding long ones, and creating bulleted lists where appropriate.

Headings of chapters can take up to as much as 1/3 of a page, creating white space to introduce the new segments.

Margins: For a book, margins are both right and left justified (as opposed to ragged edges on the right margin). Set margins at a minimum of half an inch all around. Three quarters of an inch or one inch is better. This book has one inch margins on the top and sides and three quarters on the bottom. With wider margins you can have the right and left margins the same and still accommodate binding.

Experiment with different type styles, letter sizes, letter spacing, and margins and note their impact on the number of pages and readability.

Headers and Footers: I put chapter names in the header of each page and the page numbers in the footer. By centering both, you don't have to deal with the mechanics of presenting them on either the right or left side of the page (depending on whether the page is on the right or left when the book is open). In the header, use a smaller font size than in the text. I used 9 points here. Chapter title pages should not have a header.

Page Numbers: Odd page numbers are on the right and even ones on the left. Table of contents, indexes and other sections of a book that are not the main text are often numbered with small Roman numerals. I don't do that. Blank pages should not have page numbers.

Chapters: It is common practice to begin all chapters, table of contents, introductions, indexes, and other sections of a book on the odd page number (the right page in an open book). This means the page on the left is often blank, depending on where the previous chapter ends. This is reader-friendly white space.

HINT: Study the formatting in books on hand and research formatting requirements online or in a style book, which is discussed later under "grammar."

Formatting support: Formatting is complicated for a novice, but YOU can do it. If you struggle with it and plan to write only one book, just do the writing and have someone else do the formatting. If you have an Apple computer and their support package (costs $100 a year and eliminates paying for geeks), the trainers in the store will assist you with setting up format.

Don't let this or any other mechanical process keep you from your goal of producing a biography. What you are doing is too important to be inhibited by technology.

> **HINT: To avoid being overwhelmed with learning all that is required to produce a book, break it down into time frames. Each month focus on a new skill like formatting, proofreading, photos, cover layout, printing, and anything else you need to learn. By setting a new learning objective every month or so, you build an impressive skill level over time. During this process you are interviewing, writing, and applying what you learn. Consider where you will be after a year or two--an expert at many things you can use for other applications. Looking back at how far you have come, you will be amazed at the progress.**

Editing the Format: Do the format proofing separately from proofing of text. Otherwise, you will miss things. The formatting process is different, and concentrating on text distracts from format review and vice versa.

Verify font, type style, and spacing consistency. Ensure that chapter headings tie with the table of contents, and page numbers tie with the index. Check all headings and footings. Make certain all paragraph and page breaks are proper and that margins and indentations are consistent. Look for widows and rivers and eliminate them.

GRAMMAR: You want to get this right. Here are some of the most common grammatical mistakes:

- Noun and verb don't agree
- Improper and inconsistent use of tenses
- Misuse of that, which, and who
- Confusing its with it's
- Incomplete sentences without a noun and a verb. (Sometimes this is acceptable when done for emphasis or stylistic reasons.)
- Starting a sentence with a conjunction like "and" or "but." (Sometimes you just have to.)
- Ending a sentence with a preposition. (Sometimes you just have to.)

> **HINT: A style book is a handy reference on grammar and punctuation. Strunk and White's *The Elements of Style* is considered by many to be the definitive source for style. *The Chicago Manual of Style* is popular with journalists. Amazon, libraries, and book stores offer these books and a multitude of others on the subject. There are also online sources.**

The quickest way to research grammar questions is through an online search engine. For example: Input *grammar/conjunction* or *grammar/verb noun agreement* on Google and you will get several authoritative sources, even discussion of controversial grammar issues.

The wealth of information available to a writer online is amazing. Here are examples of things I looked up through Google that demonstrate the immense value of this resource:

Is it "worse-case" or "worst-case" scenario? It is worst, although most people pronounce it worse. (Searched for: *grammar/worse-case scenario*)

How do you write in an active voice? (Searched for: *active voice vs passive voice*)

Is "silo effect" in the public domain so it can used without referencing? Yes, it is. (Searched for: *silo effect*)

Is it proper to say "backward" or "backwards"? It is backwards in England and backward in America. Either one is correct--just be consistent. (Searched for: *grammar/backwards*)

Dad said, "If you come to a fork in the road, take it." Did he make that up or did he get it from someone else? The source was Yogi Berra. (Searched by phrase: *fork in the road*)

If you can't find an answer to a grammar, punctuation, sentence structure, or spelling question, write around it.

PUNCTUATION: Oddly, there is considerable controversy around punctuation. Some of it is related to trend and some to the fact that there are English and American ways of punctuating. The important thing is to be consistent.

Wanting to be up to date, I asked a young person how to use commas these days. He said, "Don't use commas stupid." That was interesting. Another said, "Don't use any. Just use smiley faces." Someone suggested only using a comma where you pause when speaking. That's a novel approach, but if you want to do punctuation properly, go to the book store and review books on punctuation, pick a method, and stick to it.

SPELLING: Spell check is wonderful, but it will not pick up everything. If you say someone is going to "sour" instead of "soar," or you say "asses" instead of "assess," "sweat" instead of "sweet," spell check is not going to catch it.

> **HINT: To help identify spelling errors, read the text out loud and pronounce words by syllable. Some suggest reading the manuscript backwards which forces you to look at each word as distinct from the meaning of the sentence. This will reveal certain types of errors; however, it is a burdensome process which works well for shorter works but is impractical for a book.**

Your best protection against spelling, punctuation, and grammar errors is expert proofing from a fresh set of eyes, someone other than yourself.

EDITING/PROOFING: "Editing" and "proofing" are often used interchangeably, although technically editing is broader and involves rewriting and restructuring. Proofing is typically limited to looking for typos and errors in punctuation, grammar, spelling, sentence structure, and formatting. Whatever you call the process, it is critical and formidable.

Proofreading was the most tedious, challenging, and frustrating part of producing my biography, other than the technology; however, I licked the technology issue. I didn't win in the proofing arena. I found errors in my first book after it was published. Since I put so much effort into proofing and printed a large volume of books, this was a tremendous disappointment, but I learned important lessons. Two people proofed the book for me. After that, I tweaked the content. Not a good plan. I also created more errors when I fixed those found by the editors.

HINT: When you change something in the text, it is prudent to proof the whole paragraph twice, review the one before and after, and then check the formatting impact of the change throughout the chapter and the book. Also assess the impact on the index and table of

contents. Sounds burdensome. It is, but you will have mistakes if you don't do it. One change can affect many things.

In spite of all these lessons, I have not found the discipline to stop tweaking the book after it has gone to an editor. If you find errors in this text, it is not the editor's fault. Although I've come to realize that I'm not painting a Monet, I can't control the urge to make it better and no lessons have quieted my obsession. I am driven to do just one more run-through and, as a result, generate the inevitable errors. If I were a child, I would be put in time out.

Editors will tell you that they find errors in every published book, and they delight in doing so. As frustrating as that is to a writer, the important thing is that the book exists, not that it is perfect. Nevertheless, you want your book to be as polished as possible, so heavy emphasis on editing/proofing is time and effort well spent.

HINT: Print a hard copy of the drafts periodically and proof from it. Errors are easier to spot on printed paper than on a computer screen. Pick up a box of highlighters and highlight every bit of the text. I reviewed a chapter I thought was perfect this way and made thirty-eight changes, half of them blatant errors.

Amazing. The deliberate act of highlighting puts focus on each word.

It is necessary to have someone else proof your work. A fresh set of eyes will spot errors no matter how proficient you are.

Professional editors cost about $5 a page or a flat rate of around $1,500 a book. Some charge by the word. To most authors, this amount of money can make the difference between whether they will make money on their book or not, or possibly even whether they can afford to produce it. Each author must decide the amount of financial investment he is willing to make and the level of professionalism he wishes to present. You do not have to pay for proofing. Ask for support from friends, a student, or anyone strong in English and grammar. A retired school teacher friend has become a valuable resource for me.

Proofing and editing are skills that can be developed. There are books available on the subject online and in book stores. There are also classes you can take. No matter what your skill level, though, having someone else proof your manuscript is a must. My editor found sixty-one errors in a manuscript that I thought was perfect. This was after I proofed it nine times, over and over until I could find no errors.

HINT: To reduce the risk of ending up with a large quantity of books with errors, order a small number of digital copies before placing a high-volume order. Once you and others you choose to share it with have had a chance to check the book out, place the high-volume order. You don't want 500 books sitting in your garage with errors in them. Forty, not so bad.

Errors are distracting and influence the perception of the author's proficiency. You may not achieve it, but go for the perfect book and do everything you can to realize it. Just don't fret over perfection. The important thing is that you created something. Flaws are patina.

Editing Run-Throughs: Do run-throughs initially to layer on writing and polish content. In the final editing stages, do them to proof the copy and format. When you think the book is ready to go to print, make another run-through. Do that over and over until you find no errors. You will likely find yourself doing quite a number of proofing runs to get to that point.

HINT: If you start at the beginning of the book for each run-through, there will be more errors in the later chapters because you get tired and begin missing things. Start with the last chapter for a run-through and work backwards or start in

the middle. Put special emphasis on the newest and most complicated chapters.

Approach every proofing run-through with detachment, healthy skepticism, and the determined assumption that there are errors, and you are going to find them. When you think it is perfect, proof again. You will find that it is not.

HINT: Let the book bake for a few days or a week. Then do several more run-throughs. You will continue to find errors.

Then give it to someone else to proof. Double check the changes you make as a result of the editing. When I double checked the changes I made to correct the sixty-one errors my editor found, I discovered that three of them were not executed correctly and several created formatting, index, or table of contents errors.

Once you send the book to print, you will be sent a "proof" before final printing. Go over it in fine detail. Review format and text separately. Guess what. You will find errors.

By mastering writing mechanics, formatting and proofing, you acquire skills with many applications. Let's move on to another skill. Becoming a photo wizard has cross applications as well. Photos are fun, and nothing jazzes up a biography more than captivating pictures.

Chapter -6-

PHOTOS

Photos are fascinating, and when combined with words, they vividly and faithfully convey a scene or a persona. If you decide to include them, seek out a graphic designer or be prepared for another intense learning experience.

INCORPORATING PHOTOS: Getting photos into a book is a bit of a technological quagmire; however, YOU can do it. I included many photos in my biography with the help of the Apple trainers. Once you get the hang of it, working with photos is fun, and the cross application of this skill, once mastered, is expansive. Why is it such a challenge? Photos must first be digitally loaded or scanned into a computer's photo application and then installed in the book. It is a complex process.

• The photo must be sized to the space in the book. To preserve resolution, do this in the photo software before moving it to the text. Inserting photos into the text rather than dragging them in may yield better quality.

- The photo will likely require constraining or expanding and cropping.

  HINT: Ideally people's faces in photos should be at least the size of a dime.

- Other adjustments are often required to make a photo sharper, more saturated, brighter or darker, and a host of other tweaks. The quality of pictures when printed is unpredictable. Adjustments may be necessary once you see a proof copy of the book. You might consider using Photoshop software to enhance pictures.

- Printers require photos be 300 DPI resolution. The camera, scanner, and photo software play a role in making this happen. I studied this for months and never did figure it out. Graphic designers, printers, and photographers argue about it prolifically online. So what to do? I convinced a book printer to print photos "as is" and I'd accept the quality. Later I printed the same book with photos changed to the proper DPI. I couldn't tell the difference, but I now change PPI (pixels per inch) in the photo software to 600 (according to a ratio someone argued results in the required 300 DPI) and leave it at that. It seems to satisfy the printers.

• Photos must be "inlined" which means grouped with the text. Otherwise they float all over the place if you change any of the text in the book.

> **HINT: When incorporating photos in the text, always place the photo next to or after the discussion of it--never before.**

• The installation of captions below the photos requires an understanding of grouping processes that attach the caption to the picture.

• The cost of printing color pictures generally prohibits their viability for inclusion in books. Fortunately, for a biography, there is synergy to black and white photos--they imply a vintage effect. If you must have color, grouping all pictures together in a few pages to be inserted in the book by the printer reduces the cost.

> **HINT: Whether color or black and white, grouping photos together on pages separate from the text and inserting them in the center of the book simplifies the inclusion of pictures. Many books are done that way.**

PHOTO RIGHTS: Technically you should get permission from anyone living whose picture you include. Also, a photographer or someone else may have rights to a photo, in which case you must get their permission to use it, and give them credit. For their own legal protection, some printers and publishers ask you to attest to having releases from people in photos.

THE MAGIC OF PHOTOS: I included family photos in my biography. Although they could be sharper, the story would not be the same without them. It was worth the effort. This happened because I went to the Apple store for training where young geniuses advised and directed me through the process. Including photos is going to complicate things significantly, but by learning to do it, you acquire a skill that can be used in other books, newsletters, greeting cards, invitations, albums, and all manner of endeavors. Designate a month to learn the mechanics of photos. You will be glad you did. Once you understand the nuances of this process, you will be a budding, technological genius. Really.

More importantly, photographs are a gift to those who receive a biography, and they gain value with age. Years from now those photos will be quaint treasures--vintage jewels reflecting and embellishing a life story. It would not be the same without them. They are worth the effort.

You will also want to put a picture on the back cover of your book, one of yourself as the author. You might even put an old photo on the front cover that depicts the essence of your life story. Let's explore the details of designing and producing a cover.

Chapter -7-

PRODUCING A COVER

The cover is all about marketing. Once someone picks up a book or views it online, the cover is what entices them to buy it. The cover should convey what a book is about and clearly articulate the value it holds for the reader.

If you are not planning to sell your book, the cover will not need to reflect a strong marketing influence. If you do intend to sell it, making the cover a marketing marvel is an opportunity not to be missed. There are three parts to a cover, each with its own role in the overall purpose of influencing someone to want to read a book and perhaps pay money to do so:

The front...sparks interest and clearly articulates what the book is about through artwork, the title, sub-title, and other points.

The spine...is what most people see when the book is on a shelf. Executing it well is immensely important. (A small book may not have a spine.)

129

The back...is marketing, marketing, marketing which enthusiastically and blatantly conveys the compelling qualities of the book. Glowing reviews and a picture and short bio of the author round out the back cover.

TECHNICALITIES OF COVER DESIGN: You will likely need graphic design support for producing the cover layout. Additionally, input from a marketing or public relations friend is helpful for developing content.

Freelance graphic designers can be hired for around $500-$1,000. Printers often provide cover design support. Costs and quality can vary substantially. CreateSpace, owned by Amazon, offers this service (*createspace.com*). With the right software and a willingness to learn, you can do it yourself. There is a significant learning curve to becoming proficient; however, once this skill is acquired, you can design brochures, business cards, stationary, newsletters, invitations, greeting cards, and even a website.

> **HINT: Apple trainers will teach you to use their graphic design software.**

Fonts and artwork on the cover need special attention. Amateur efforts often look, well, they look amateur. Publishers or printers who offer cover design may deliver cookie cutter or poor artistic quality, even though they charge a lot for it. (More about that in *Chapters 8* and *9*.) Your best bet is a freelance graphic designer or a friend or family member who knows graphic design. You can take coursework in graphic design if that interests you and develop a creative skill with many cross applications.

> **HINT: A writers' group in your area can direct you to a local graphic designer who has experience with book covers.**

For a biography, a vintage looking photo on the front cover can be interesting. I used one of me on a tractor for *Out of Iowa*. Designer fonts add a professional touch to any writing on the cover.

> **HINT: Photos for covers can be purchased at online sites such as *dreamtime.com*. Artful *Garamond* fonts and popular cover fonts League Gothic, Chunk Five, Birra, Coda, and Matchbook are good choices. (Google: *fonts*)**

The front, back, and spine of a cover are designed on one wrap-around sheet in a "layout file," as distinguished from a word processing file where the text resides.

The layout margins must extend at least a fourth of an inch outside the bounds of the book to accommodate what printers call the bleed. The excess is required because they must run the background color past the book's edge and then trim off the excess cover card stock.

Do the cover in softback as opposed to hardback. Hard covers are much more expensive and require a sleeve, another major design step. Although some people still value hardbacks, most don't want to pay for them, and those who travel prefer the lighter weight and less bulk of a softback. The trend is clearly toward softback.

Color covers have become standard in the industry. The extra cost is minimal. (Color within the text can run up costs considerably, but on the cover there is little or no difference between the cost of color as opposed to black and white.) Colors are tricky. There can be a significant difference between what a color looks like on the computer screen and what ends up on the printed cover. There are also color variances between digital and offset printing. This is important to know because proofs are digital even if the final book is offset.

HINT: Colors will generally appear brighter and lighter on the computer screen than in print.

The only way to guarantee a precise color is to use the standard *Pantone* colors which have code numbers that are industry standard. A local printer can show you a sample color chart of these standard colors. Companies use them to guarantee that their logos are always printed in the exact color. You can give these color numbers to some printers and be more certain of the end result, but not all printers will do that. (Many printers run a number of different book covers at one time, which restricts the capability to tweak the color for one book.)

FRONT COVER: The front cover is all about conveying what the book is about and creating interest in reading it.

Title: The title of a book is crucial if you publish because the words in titles are used by search engines to find books. Amazon, libraries, and bookstores search by key words in titles and subtitles. For example, my biography is titled *Out of Iowa.* It will pop up if anyone does a search on Iowa. By adding *Into Oklahoma* as a subtitle, I doubled the geographical marketing audience. Cram as many key words as possible into the title and any other writing on the front cover. This is challenging because, for good design, concise and efficient wording is required.

If you are producing a book to give to family and friends as opposed to publishing and selling, key words are not so important, but whether you publish or not, the title should generate interest. Think of it as a "hook," something crisp, captivating, memorable, catchy, and easy to remember that draws the reader in and keeps him engaged. Use this phrase on the cover and throughout the book. It represents a theme, the primary message of the book.

Keep the title to no more than 45 characters, or have the first few words conducive to searching. (Some book registers are limited to 45 characters.) Also, keep it short enough to fit on the spine in large print, or at least structure the title so the first few words are appropriate for the spine.

Subtitle: This, too, should include key words for searching and provide detail on what the book is about. Amazon searches by subtitle.

Other Verbiage: There is room on the front cover for a few other remarks. The word "memoir," "biography," or "life story" and the subject's name somewhere on the cover articulates what and whom the book is about. Keep marketing in mind when deciding what to include. What can you say in a few words about what is inside that will make a person want to read the book? For a biography, search for something that sums up the person. For *Out of Iowa* I put the following theme on the cover:

> You can take the girl out of Iowa, but
> You can't take the Iowa out of the girl.

It reflects what the book is about--growing up in Iowa and how that affected the rest of my life.

The author's name should be prominent on the front of the book. The publishing company name can be there and/or on the spine.

SPINE: The title of the book and the author's last name should be prominent on the spine. Libraries and book stores file books by authors' last names. The name of the publishing company may also be included. The spine is what people see if the book is on a bookshelf. The color and an intriguing, crisp title in large, readable letters are what make a book stand out from the rest and encourage shoppers to pull it out and look at it. Make the spine an attention grabber.

The size of the spine must be calculated at some point while designing the cover. It is determined by the number of pages and the weight of the text paper. A printer can help ascertain spine size, or you can find formulas online by Googling "book covers/spine." A 280-page book will typically have a half inch spine. (Spine size can be estimated by measuring books with similar pages and paper weight.)

BACK COVER: You must lose your sense of modesty and rave about yourself and your book on the back cover. Study books in the bookstore or library for a flavor of how to lay it on in a concise, convincing manner.

Write as if you are the publisher talking about the book and author. Describe what the reader will get out of the book. Emphasize lessons and entertainment value. Use emotional power words and incorporate hooks.

A picture of you as the author is a nice touch. Put your fear of vanity aside and promote both your book and yourself as the author. That is what it is all about, and people want to visualize the person who wrote the book as they are reading it. This makes it more real and meaningful. Brand yourself as an author with your name and a professional photo.

To sell a book, you must have a bar code on the back cover (more about that later).

Even if you are not planning to sell the book, the more professional you make it and the more it looks like a "real" book, the more it is impressive for generations to come. A polished, quality book with a wonderful cover honors the life of the person you write about, whether it is you or someone else.

REVIEWS: Because the cover is a sales tool, the back is often where reviews are placed. They can also be in the first few pages of the book, or both. If you are going to sell the book, you may want to seek reviews, but it is a lot of work and is not required. It is preferable to use reviewers with impressive credentials or titles. Reviews should be limited to two or three sentences.

HINT: If you are not planning to sell the book, there can be considerable entertainment value in getting reviews from relatives and friends of the person you are writing about. If they don't have time to read the book, suggest they give a short testimonial about the person. Seek out the quick-witted jokesters and the older folks. These playful reviews will add unexpected charm and amusement to the book. Those providing the reviews will feel involved and vested in your project. Help them edit their comments down to two or three sentences.

It is a big favor to ask someone to invest the time required to read your book and give a review. It also adds considerable time to the publishing time frame. You must get drafts to people and wait for them to read it (some will never get it done) and get back to you with comments. You must then edit them into short review statements and add them to the book.

I decided not to deal with soliciting reviews for my biography, so I fabricated ridiculous ones. I disclosed in small print that they

137

were made up and that "Sometimes I do things I shouldn't."

Consider ways to make the style of the cover consistent with the character and tone of the book. I explored several colors when creating the *Out of Iowa* book cover and nothing clicked until I tried green. It is not one of my favorite colors, but when I plugged it into the design, I knew immediately that was the color. I tweaked it to the shade of the dark leaves in the fields of corn that cover the Iowa landscape in summer.

Probably nothing is more important about your book than the cover. Few will read the text if the cover does not appeal to them. Make it so captivating that when you hand it to someone they are fascinated. That is a big order, but the cover is everything to a book.

To realize the wow factor on a cover, you must deliver the goods on printing. This requires some serious decision making, and those decisions determine how crazy wonderful the book will be or what disappointments await you. Printing brings a book to life. It also thrusts you into a precarious dance with vendors. This requires that you know what you are doing because they may step on your toes. Let's explore printing.

Chapter -8-

PRINTING

Once the text and cover are developed, it is time to actually produce the book. This means printing it. To be a savvy book producer, you've got to nail the printing.

If the book is to be distributed to family, friends, and other direct contacts, you can simply print it and get it out. If you plan to sell it on the open market, you are entering the world of publishing, which introduces many complications to printing. Before we get into that, though, let's talk about the basic printing issues that apply to everyone whether they are selling or not.

After months, maybe years, of working on a book, you will wonder if it is ever finished. It is difficult to know when to pull the plug and go to print. Polishing and enhancing is a never-ending process. With every run-through the book gets better. As you look back after each pass and realize how much improvement was made, you are glad you didn't stop and print. As a result, you know it will be even better if you keep going, so you become hesitant to ever consider it finished. At some point, though, you must cease creating and produce the book. Once you do, you may have regrets about things you didn't get in it or something not developed or polished enough.

HINT: This is not a catastrophe. Order small quantities at first, even if they cost more per copy. Make notes of changes and put out a more polished edition later.

The importance of understanding the printing process is brought home when reflecting on cost. You don't want to make mistakes and have a bunch of defective books lying around in which you have invested a lot of money.

Printing is a big component of the cost of producing a book, running about $2,000 for five hundred 280-page books or $1,200 for two hundred. You can get fifty books for somewhere around $400. Fewer pages and lower quality paper bring costs down. Prices fluctuate significantly between vendors.

If on top of that you hire an editor for $1,000 and a graphic designer for $1,000, and pay to distribute the book, you begin to see the challenges of making money on it. The average self-published book sells 200 copies, and only 5% of books published ever recover expenses. That is reality.

Be smart about selecting a printing vendor and getting the best deal possible. Over and above the deal, you need to know how printers compete for business. Some routinely take advantage of writers. To avoid this, you must understand how this industry works.

INDUSTRY TRENDS: The printing and publishing industries are in unprecedented flux. The internet, electronic distribution channels, digital printing, and innovative marketing models are re-shaping these industries. Influence has shifted from publishers and agents to aspiring writers who can now self-publish, and they are doing so in droves. In spite of this new-found power, writers are being taken advantage of as vendors play on their naiveté and unrealistic dreams.

When seeking a printer, you will run into companies that are not just printers. They want to publish your book. This is precarious territory for the novice. Although self-publishing is a boon for writers, it is forcing them to face the intricacies of the business of book production, distribution, and marketing. Be skeptical of package deals offered by those pursuing their piece of the self-publishing pie--your money.

HINT: Those offering royalties, registering the book in their name, and using their logo

are not just printing your book. They are publishing it. You are no longer the publisher. This may not be a good thing, depending on your goals and who you are dealing with. There are scammers out there. More about that in *Chapter 9*.

PRINTING METHODS - OFFSET/DIGITAL: There are two basic methods of printing: *offset* and *digital*. Offset yields the best quality and the lowest cost per book but has large set-up costs, so offset printers typically require a minimum order of 500 copies. Offset also takes the most time. Digital printing, on the other hand, is quick and conducive to small quantities, but it is more expensive per book and the quality might be less. As you learn about the types of printing vendors, the attributes and consequences of these two methods are revealed.

OFFICE SERVICE STORES: Stores such as Kinkos can produce attractive 8 1/2 x 11 spiral or tape bound books with card stock covers in a short time frame. Rather than binding, the pages can be three-hole punched and put in notebooks, some with clear covers in which a printed page can be inserted to serve as the cover. This is digital printing. Orders are placed online at *printonlinekinkos.com* or you can take a flash drive into the store with the files. Create a simple cover in the text file (perhaps incorporating a photo) and eliminate the need for a separate layout file. This simplifies things.

This is the easiest approach, but probably the most expensive of the options. A 200-page book will run around $30 per copy, but if you are printing a few copies just for family and friends, this might be your best bet.

> **HINT: Order one copy to check things out before ordering multiple copies.**

LOCAL PRINTERS: Many local print shops can print a professional looking book with either digital or offset. They may contract out the binding (Most local print shops don't do binding.) This increases costs and delays delivery. If you go this route, consider getting quotes from several printers. Prices can vary greatly. You may pay around $10 per book, not a bad price for a gift for family and friends, but if you sell the book, a profit is unlikely at this cost.

OFFSET BOOK PRINTERS: These are large, often venerable companies that set the standard. Specializing in producing books in high volumes, they typically will not print fewer than 500 books, but they are usually the cheapest per book and deliver the best quality. It is unlikely offset will be a good choice for you because you won't want to print huge volumes, but as a writer, you need to have some knowledge of it.

You might pay about the same amount for five hundred *offset* books as you pay for a couple of hundred *digital* ones. The downside of this is that if there is something wrong with the book, you've got 500 of them.

> In case you want to know what five hundred copies of a 250-page book delivered on a pallet looks like, it takes up space equivalent to the size of a small to average sized desk.

If you think you will sell or give that many books away eventually and storage is not a problem, high-volume offset printing may be the best bargain. Volume price breaks bring the price per book down significantly although the cash outlay is substantial. Here is an example of common offset printing pricing:

Offset Printing

Books	Each	Total
500	$3.80	$1,900
1,000	2.30	2,300
2,000	1.60	3,100
3,000	1.35	4,000

You can find offset vendors through Google. I used *Central Plains Book Manufacturing* in Kansas and got a quality book at a decent price.

Although offset printers have historically been the industry standard, the quality of digital printing is improving. It is probably the best choice for you because it is unlikely you will want to order 500 offset books. The digital printing arena, though, is a precarious place for novice writers. Here is why.

PRINT ON DEMAND DIGITAL PRINTERS: The print on demand (POD) name is a bit of a misnomer because most of these vendors are much more than digital printers, offering many add-on services and publishing functions. This may appear to be a good thing at first blush, but it has created a virtual mine field for writers.

These new guys on the block have propelled both the printing and publishing industries into a state of flux--revolutionizing them by giving writers access to a new and efficient channel to get books out. This POD business model emerged as a key player because of its relationship to another new kid on the block, online book retailers (companies like Amazon and Barnes & Noble). This connection has provided POD companies a seat at the online sales table by providing printing and fulfillment (packaging and shipping) for those sales.

The problem is the array of other services offered which are often not financially viable and that tread on the author's rights to his work.

Many authors believe they are self-publishing when using POD vendors, and frequently they are not. That is the result of vendor hype, writer ignorance, and the intricacies of the business. More about that in *Chapter 9 - Publishing*.

POD companies typically offer many tempting services: design, editing, printing, fulfillment, copyrighting, registering, publishing, marketing, distribution, and more. Prices may be outrageously high, contracts can be restricting, and quality suspect. The potpourri of POD business models is blurring the lines between printing and publishing, which has caused many a confused writer to shell out money expecting unrealistic outcomes. Also, a writer may unknowingly limit his future options through exclusive contracts and jeopardize a book's acceptance because a company put its label (logo) on the book. Worst of all, an author may unwisely give up the rights to his work.

Among POD printers, competition is keen and marketing to writers aggressive--playing on unrealistic hopes and dreams. When you access these companies' websites or put contact information on a public record (copyright, Library of Congress, book registry), be prepared for an onslaught of marketing solicitation.

Your best bet initially is to use POD companies only to digitally print the book and ship it to you for direct sales to your contacts. Printers suggest enticing deals. You should do some serious strategic planning and perform a detailed cost/benefit analysis before taking one. If you decide to sell a book, determine the optimal approach for you, not for a company after your money.

POD Print and Deliver To You: This is a scenario where it makes sense for you to use POD printing, which has filled the gap left by offset printers (who will typically not print fewer than 500 copies) by offering low volume printing. This involves simply having them digitally print books and ship to you. Read the small print in any printing agreement.

I've gotten the best digital prices and quality printing from CreateSpace which is owned by Amazon. They guide new writers through the process of printing and make books available on Amazon, Kindle, and Apple products. Their production services (cover design and editing) are reasonably priced, and the website (*createspace.com*) is loaded with helpful educational information for novice writers.

Digital printers may require a minimum order of forty or so books. Although the price per book will be less than local store printing, it is usually higher than offset. However, you are not buying a lot of books so dollars spent are less in total.

HINT: Don't let printing companies put their logo on your book. They are not publishing the book--they are just printing it. More about this in *Chapter 9*.

I used a couple of small POD companies for rush digital printing with good results, although one left a rough edge on the cover, substantiating claims that sometimes quality suffers with these companies. I've stayed away from the larger companies that pester me with phone calls and insist on putting their logo on the book.

✳✳✳✳✳✳✳✳✳✳✳

If you don't intend to sell your book, most of the rest of this chapter will not apply to you. It is helpful information, though, because once you reach out to printers, you are going to experience some of the complications of the industry whether they apply to you or not. Knowledge is your friend.

✳✳✳✳✳✳✳✳✳✳✳

POD Printing and Fulfillment: The basic concept of print on demand is that a book is digitally printed only when someone buys it, virtually eliminating inventory management and costs. Digital printing can produce a single book quickly and at a viable cost.

In combination with online book retailers like Amazon, POD companies seamlessly print, sell, and distribute books. The seller (Amazon) markets to buyers, accepts orders, collects and distributes money, and records sales. The POD company prints, packages, and ships the books. Both companies take a cut of the sale. Amazon puts the writer's share of the sale in an account and periodically transfers it to his bank and pays the POD company for printing and fulfillment.

If and when you decide to sell a book online, you might avail yourself of POD print and fulfillment services, but you need to get educated first. Vendor selection is crucial. Many market services to you that are not cost effective. Bundling services into a package makes them appealing, but before contracting for anything more than basic printing, you need a well-thought out strategy, unless you don't care whether you get a return. There is a huge variance between vendors in both cost and quality. I use CreateSpace to provide printed copies to me for my direct sales, to print and fulfill online Amazon book orders, and to format and connect to Kindle for electronic book sales.

Printers may cross over into publishing. This is where things get complicated. Most POD companies are not just printers. Perhaps they are technically not publishers, either, but they are darn close. Further complicating the issue, some businesses that are in all aspects publishers masquerade as POD companies in order to play on writers' attraction to the self-publishing trend. As I said, it is a mine field out there.

Large national POD printers have taken a jack-of-all-trades approach by offering many services, aggressively marketing them, and brilliantly packaging them in ways that entice naive authors to part with their money for a comprehensive plan to turn their book into a big seller. As a consumer, be smart about dealing with them, no matter how they label themselves. Most companies focus on getting as many writers as possible to sign up. That is where their revenue comes from, not from sales of the writers' books.

Book Production Services: For a fee, many printing companies offer author services, which include such production tasks as editing, cover design, formatting, and photo insertion. You can spend a lot of money here. Prices are often inflated and the quality of work inconsistent. If you have no other sources, these services can help make your book a reality, but pore over any contracts thoroughly and understand every provision and the small print. Do a cost/benefit analysis. Don't sign away the rights to your book or the artwork on the cover, the right to use another printer, or the right to cancel at will. In general, it's better to use local freelancers for book development services, although I've found CreateSpace to be cost effective.

Wholesaler/Retailer Connections: Print companies may urge you to pay them to get your book listed on wholesaler listings like Ingram,

Baker & Taylor, and Bertram, implying that retail stores like Barnes and Noble and libraries can then buy your book. Getting on a listing does not mean retail book stores, libraries, or anyone else will buy it. They probably won't.

Online Sales Connections: Printing companies may propose that you pay them to get your book on an online book sales site. If you choose to do this, seek a deal where you don't stand to lose a lot of money if sales don't materialize (no large upfront fees). Review contracts carefully. *Chapter 9* includes a checklist of what to watch out for when procuring services.

Check out CreateSpace for the connection to online Amazon sales and to Kindle and Apple's electronic books. This can be a solid marketing opportunity with small upfront costs. Unfortunately, CreateSpace will not get you on all the major eBook devices or all wholesaler lists, but those may not be your target markets anyway. No vendor is likely to have everything a self-publishing author needs, and multiple vendors may be required to meet broad marketing goals, a reason to avoid exclusive arrangements in any contracts.

Electronic Interfaces: Books must be re-formatted for eBooks. For a fee and/or a cut of all future eBook sales, some printers offer to do the formatting and install the interface to electronic devices such as Kindle, Nook, iBooks, and Sony Reader. Electronic books are no doubt the wave of the future. In fact, some experts advise that authors skip the printed form and go directly to the electronic books sales channel.

CreateSpace can hook you up to to Kindle and Apple's iBooks. Smashwords is a company that does re-formatting and interface for a broad range of electronic devices, including Barnes and Noble's Nook. Both vendors take a cut of the sales price. (You can avoid the middleman and do the eBook connection yourself, but the re-formatting requirements alone made my head hurt. You'd have to be a technical genius with lots of time to pull it off. You could write another book instead.)

Printers Offering Marketing Services: If you plan to sell a book, odds are slim that a printing company's marketing services are cost effective. A cost benefit analysis is unlikely to prove them viable because average book sales over the life of a book, regardless of who does the marketing, is only 200 copies. A harsh, but true reality.

Biographies are niche books, a fact which further narrows the market. In addition, the net profit per book is shockingly small. Keep these points in mind when vendor hype promises to make your book a raging success. Their revenue will most likely come from you, not from sales.

Books are almost always sold at a discount, often a hefty one. You may price a book at $15, but it sells for $6. Whether this impacts what you get depends on the formula the seller uses to pay you. Regardless of how that is calculated, once the seller and a print and fulfillment company take their cuts, there is little left for you. You may sell 200 books and end up with a few hundred dollars.

For a price, many printers promote books through their own newsletters, reviewers, review publications, and online promotion vehicles. These are not customized marketing programs and are unlikely to spur meaningful sales, especially for a memoir. Don't be lured into deals that are not lucrative. There is a universal truth in this business. **No matter what business model you choose for sales and distribution (an agent, major traditional publisher, print on demand, online sales, eBooks, or a combination of these), you, as the author, must market the book if a significant sales volume is to be generated.**

When you pay someone to market, they get your money, so they are guaranteed a profit. You, on the other hand, are extremely unlikely to get your investment back, let alone make anything. You are taking all the risk, and they are getting the sure deal--your money.

HINT: Companies often ask for your email contact list and the names and addresses of friends and relatives. DON'T GIVE IT TO THEM. Sell to these people direct. Why should you give those easy sales to anyone else? Why should you give anyone a cut of the revenue from your own sources? Your contacts are a huge portion of the 200 books you are likely to sell. Keep them for yourself.

Lets talk about these direct sales, your best opportunity to make money and recoup costs of book production because of the profit margin.

Printing for Direct Sales: These are sales you make yourself to people with whom you are in direct contact or through your own website. It is the optimal sales opportunity; you pay for printing but no one else gets a cut. There is no middleman. To do this, you need a supply of books in your possession.

Regardless of any arrangement made for printing and fulfillment for online retail sales, print a supply of books to store, sell, and distribute yourself. Print them for around $5 each. Sell them through book clubs, your website, or directly to friends, relatives, and contacts for $15 and realize a nice $10 profit. **To be able to sell direct, you must not give anyone exclusive**

rights to print or sell your book. (Red flags should go up any time you hear the words "rights" or "exclusive" or see them in a contract or an agreement of any kind.)

If you are planning to sell a biography or any other book, buy books on publishing and marketing and do online research before developing your printing, publishing, and marketing strategy. Your best source of information is other authors, not POD or publishing companies. After reading many books on self-publishing, I recommend these two, which I found to be the most comprehensive and objective sources for publishing intelligence. Both are written by seasoned authors:

The Complete Guide to Self-Publishing
by Marilyn Ross and Sue Collier
Everything you need to know to write, publish, promote, and sell your own book.

The Essential Guide
to Getting Your Book Published
by Arielle Eckstut and David Henry Sterry
How to write it, sell it, and market it...successfully!

PRINTING THE COVER: The biggest challenge to printing the cover is getting the colors right. What you see on the computer screen may not be what you get when the proof arrives. Also, what you see on the proof may not be what you get with the final product either, another reason to order smaller quantities.

COATINGS: Have a coating put on the cover. If you do not, the color will peel off if the cover is bent or when books rub together in shipping. Laminate or UV coatings are the most common and come in glossy or matte, with glossy the most popular.

COST QUOTES: If you plan to sell your book and are going to print a large volume, get quotes from several printers. Google "book printers" to identify potential vendors. Most printer websites will let you input printing specifications. They then send a quote by email.

Ask for quotes for several volumes so you can assess price break points. For offset, breaks are usually at 500/1000/2000/3000. Most digital printing companies will do any volume, although some might have a minimum of forty or so. Particularly with offset, the per unit cost declines substantially with volume orders. This makes an order of 3,000 at $1.35 a book tempting, which is the equivalent of five or six desks in your garage, depending on the size of the book. Keep in mind that statistically the likelihood of your selling 500 books is remote, and printing small volumes digitally gives you the flexibility to reprint with enhancements later. By shopping printers, you can order a hundred or so digital copies for about $5 each and avoid the potential waste of a large volume offset order.

> **HINT: Nothing is worse than to receive a thousand books and find something wrong with them. Test out a book before making a large volume offset investment by ordering a small number of digital copies first.**

Climate controlled storage is recommended for books; however, I've experienced no problems storing books with laminated covers in the garage, and I've hauled them around in the trunk of my car in hot Oklahoma weather with no consequences.

PRINTING SPECIFICATIONS: To solicit a print bid, you must provide specifications. Here is a sample of specs and questions you should ask when seeking quotes for printing:

> Pages: 256
> Number of Copies: 500/1000
> Size of book: 6 x 9
> Cover 10 point weight
> UV or Laminate Coating - Glossy
> Text 60# white*
> Perfect Binding
> Offset or Digital?
> Overrun cost?
> Proof fees?

Change fees?

Freight?

Sales Tax?**

Delivery Time Frame?

Accept Credit Card?

No printer logo on book?

*If less than 50# paper, photos might bleed through.

**If you are going to sell the book, you can
  get an exemption.

The *overrun cost* is a standard industry practice in offset printing whereby you are charged for any extra copies produced in the printing process. If you want 500 and they send you 60 more for the overrun, you have to pay for them, probably at a discount. (Overruns should not occur with digital printing.) Lighter pound and lower grade text paper is available, and it may cost less, but check for ink bleed-through, especially on photos. Cover weight can be reduced, but the covers may curl.

Printers often charge for any changes they have to make to the electronic files you send. This is an unpredictable cost. At $25 to $100 per change, it can quickly add up. (CreateSpace does not charge for changes.) There can be other hidden costs which make it difficult to compare vendors. Look for the small print in bid responses. The extras add up--soon a $1,600 quote is a $2,300 charge.

HINT: The printing market is competitive. You have leverage. Ask for no overrun fees. Negotiate away or put a limit on charges for changes after a proof. If someone else beats a vendor's price, ask him to meet it.

You must submit your book to the printer electronically, usually in PDF format. The text and cover are submitted in separate files because the cover is a layout file as opposed to text.

PROOFS: Don't skip the proofing step. Request a proof and review every page thoroughly before printing. The printer can get a proof to you in three or four days. It will be a digital sample of the text and cover, possibly unbound. You may be charged for changes made as the result of the proof review, so do intense editing before submitting files to a printer.

HINT: After reviewing proofs, ask to make changes yourself and re-submit the files rather than paying a printer to make them. (CreateSpace allows re-submissions.)

DELIVERY: Once changes identified from the proof review are implemented, the book is ready to print. You should have it in about three weeks.

I ordered 500 offset copies of my first book. (I don't recommend doing that many.) The day they were delivered, a large semi pulled up in front of the house. The air brakes hissed, and I went to the window to observe a truck too large to get into the garage area. The driver said, "No problem. I have a fork lift." As I opened the garage door, he came at me on the fork lift with boxes of books on a wooden pallet.

After he deposited them, along with the pallet, I stood there alone, staring at the mound of boxes thinking: "Holy cow. This is going to be a problem for my children when I die." Although it was overwhelming, it was a defining moment. After tearing into the first box, I got my hands on a copy of my first book and thought to myself: "I am published. I am an author."

Printing creates something tangible--a book. Publishing is the mechanism for selling it. Even if you don't anticipate selling, the next chapter on publishing includes warnings about scammers who are adept at targeting writers to tempt with enticing proposals. You'll want to know about that. You may not be looking for them, but they will be looking for you.

- III. -

PUBLISHING A

BIOGRAPHY

Through your writing,
The past connects with the future,
Generations link together in a common thread,
And a legacy is created.

Chapter -9-

PUBLISHING

The publishing arena is where a book is promoted and sold. It requires a publishing company, your own if you decide to self-publish. Again, unless you plan to sell a biography on the open market, there is no reason to publish. Just print and you're done. Family members can kick in on the cost of printing, but if you cross the line into selling a book to the general public, you are entering the realm of publishing.

There are basically three tracks to publishing: *traditional* publishers (major or mid-sized, established publishing houses and small specialty publishers), *vanity* publishers, and the modern trend of *self-publishing*.

TRADITIONAL PUBLISHERS: This is the golden ring if you can get it. Although it is a myth that the major publishing houses are not interested in first-time authors, competition between authors is keen, and there are hundreds of thousands of novice writers. Getting a blockbuster-focused, traditional publisher to accept your biography is an extreme long shot, and you will have little or no control over book development and publishing processes if they do. The upside is that you don't have to front the money to publish and you are dealing with the industry standard--the big leagues.

VANITY PUBLISHERS: These businesses require that you front all the money to produce a book, including the publisher's profit which, by the way, is most of the money you give them. Subsidy publishers are a variation of vanity publishers. They share in the up front money but generally recoup their investment before you recoup yours. Because of industry prejudices, neither of these are likely to label themselves as what they are. You have to figure it out. Your giving them money is what distinguishes them most. They are the publishers of last resort, and experts generally advise avoiding them.

SELF-PUBLISHING: This is a sure way to get a book out and maintain control of the process, if you are careful. It is work and requires that you understand the industry. You are essentially running a business and must spend your time and money to get the book published, but you cut out the middlemen. You don't have to share profits if you follow the pure self-publishing model.

True self-publishing requires that you form a publishing company, maintain all rights to your

164

work, secure the editing, cover design, layout, printing, and shipping, set the price, and determine marketing strategy.

The self-publisher may contract with vendors to perform some of these functions. Under this scenario, the author can lose control of these processes and possibly the rights to his work even though he is the publisher, or at least thinks he is. This is why understanding the business is vital. It is one reason industry prejudices ascribed to vanity publishing extend to the self-publishing model (you may think you are the publisher, but you are not). Others reasons are that novice self-publishers sometimes don't know what they are doing, make mistakes that complicate the production process, deliver a sub-standard book, and aren't professional.

Under none of the three publishing scenarios (traditional, vanity/subsidy, and self-publishing) are you likely to experience a substantial income stream, and under the vanity option, where you are providing the front money to the publisher, you are almost certain to lose money. It's a complex industry and the most formidable aspect of it is figuring out into which category publishers and printing vendors fit. For this reason, you need to study up.

HINT: When searching for books on publishing, be aware that some are written

by those who have a vested interest in a company that prints and markets books. These books are biased. Companies may encourage employees or contacts to post rave reviews of their "how to" books on online sites and post bad reviews of books published by competing companies. (It is a bit of a jungle out there.) Consider the source of all information. Your best sources are other writers. The books mentioned in *Chapter 8* **are objective sources written by writers. There are many more.**

If there is a part of the process of being a writer that requires managing expectations, publishing is it. Fantasies of the naive can lead to unfortunate circumstances. Most writers harbor unrealistic dreams of fame and fortune from a national best seller. If you have such grand illusions, you need a reality check. A plethora of scammers stand ready to play on those hopes in order to get you to part with your money.

The reality is that there are over a million writers in this country from whom approximately 300,000 books are published each year. Only about 5% of them result in significant sales. Most of those are from established authors or famous people. **For unknown authors, the average number of books sold is 200, and a best selling book is an extreme long shot. High selling**

biographies, unless they are about famous people, are even more of an anomaly.

Glory stories of authors getting rich represent a minuscule portion of the writing population, but they are highly publicized. Stories of self-publishing being a springboard to getting picked up by a major publishing company are exaggerated. Simply stated, it is possible but extremely unlikely your book will be a big seller. If you find this disheartening, consider this:

> Chase your writing dreams, but be honest about why you do it. Most writers don't write to get rich, although we dream about that. We write because we love to create. We relish seeing what we write blossom into a beautiful book that is shared. In the case of biography, we do it to create a legacy--to reveal a life story to generations to come. **It is not about the money.**

PUBLISHING OPTIONS: Historically the road to publishing a book was the same for everyone. It required getting the attention of a large to medium-sized traditional publisher (a major, established publishing house), perhaps through a literary agent. This involved considerable time, effort, determination, and a very thick skin.

Worse yet, it might not be achievable, which meant the book would not be shared. On the up side, under this scenario, the writer did not front any money. The publisher financed and produced the book, taking his cut from sales. The author received royalties--a percentage of sales. In spite of the drawbacks, it was a good gig, if you could get it. Very few could.

Rejected authors were forced to use vanity publishers who required them to front the money to publish a book. (The up front money required from the author is what distinguishes a vanity company from a traditional publisher.) This guarantees the publisher his profit whether the book sells or not, so he has little incentive to sell it. Most retail book stores shun these books, and the author gets measly royalties on the few sales generated. Additionally, he has to pay for any books he wants for his own purposes (more profit for the vanity publisher), and possibly loses the rights to his work. A host of other unfortunate outcomes can occur. Rejected by traditional publishers, this was historically a writer's only option.

Now, the new publishing model has shuffled the deck and changed the publisher's playpen to a writer's wonderland. Self-publishing, made attractive by online book stores, electronic books, and digital printing, has revolutionized the publishing industry and unleashed the print on demand phenomenon. Along with the advantages of this model, problems for writers emerged because of the sea of choices and because the lines between true self-publishing and vanity publishing have been blurred. Authors are vulnerable and think they are self-publishing when they are not.

True self-publishers are often referred to as "indies." They are independent. Bona fide self-publishing requires that an author form a publishing company, own the ISBN of his books, and is listed as the owner of record on the *Books in Print Register.* The copyright and Library of Congress registrations are in his name, his publishing company is printed on the book (as opposed to another company's logo), and he holds all rights to it. He may contract for printing, fulfillment (packaging and delivery), and other services but he avoids exclusive arrangements. An indie normally sets the retail price. He may contract to share the proceeds of sales with a print vendor or a book seller.

In contrast, when a writer allows POD or vanity companies to take ownership of rights and gives them an exclusive to provide services, he is no longer a true self-publisher by the literal definition. Approximately 80% of books produced are published outside of the traditional publishing category, but they are such a blend of vanity and self-publishing that it is impossible to determine how many are actually self-published.

You can be the publisher. YOU can do it. Whether you can sell the book or make any money once you publish it is another story, and that is exactly why the major and mid-sized traditional publishing companies are unlikely to pick up your book. Being blockbuster-centric, they are going after the sure thing. In contrast, the vanity publishers (some of them labeled POD companies) want to get hold of you because they know they can make money on your book whether it is marketable or not because you give them their profit up front.

Since getting a traditional publishing company to publish a book is a remote prospect and vanity companies are in disfavor, true self-publishing is a hot trend. POD companies print and provide fulfillment, and an online sales company like Amazon sells it and handles the exchange of money. Some POD companies offer formatting services and interfaces required to get a book to the electronic reader market. This is good news and bad news. You must pay for these services, and/or they take a cut of sales revenue. As a steward of your publishing company, do a thorough analysis of any offerings that require upfront money or a cut of the sales.

It is discouragingly complex, but don't let the complications of the publishing business keep you from realizing your writing dreams. You don't have to dabble in all of this. You can narrow your scope to avoid the pitfalls, but you do need to be aware of them because vanity and subsidy companies will be seeking you out.

Become your own best advocate by learning the business and be grateful for the self-publishing mechanisms available today, which assure what you write is shared. Aspire to produce beautiful books, recoup as much as possible of the cost of doing so, and enjoy being an author. If you happen to make money in the process, celebrate. You are the exception to the rule.

Considering the time and effort an author must spend writing and producing a book, odds are he could spend this time at a second job and realize much more income. If this is the case, why do so many people do it? It is not about the money. It is about why we write--the creation, the artistry, and, in the case of biography, it is about capturing life and, most importantly, sharing it.

SCAMMERS: Don't take any steps to publish until you understand how the bottom feeders of this business work. There are a lot of them trying to make a few bucks from the thousands of hopeful writers with dreams of selling great quantities of books.

These guys track you down through your online searches, registrations, and copyrights and aggressively pursue getting you to send them money. A few claim to be Christian companies, implying a level of trust they don't deserve. Many make promises they don't keep. Don't be a victim of the fantasies of the uninformed. Use due diligence to check out companies and offers, or better yet, ignore them. Scammers don't take risks. With the exception of a few measly royalties, money flows from you to them. You are writing the checks. Here is how they work.

They typically ask for a copy of your manuscript. Then they notify you that it is remarkable (which is what they tell everyone) and request a substantial amount of money. You send them $4,000 to $10,000. They've got to sell a lot of books for you to get your money back. Can they do that? Highly unlikely. Do the math.

Under most of these arrangements, you have to buy from them any books you want after you've already fronted the money to print them. What is wrong with this picture? Further, it is unlikely they invest in printing many copies. They know they are not going to sell any except those your friends and family buy, if they can con you out of your contact list. When you realize the book is not selling, they ask for more money to fund more promotion, and many people give it to them. Don't be one of those people.

When using a search engine like Google to find book printers, a slew of companies will appear wearing the POD label. This model is impossible to define because there are so many variations of it, and many of them are a form of vanity publishers. Some non-vanity companies might be okay to print digital books for your direct sales and for fulfilling Amazon or other online sales orders, but sorting through them is frustrating.

As a self-publisher, rather than sifting through all these companies, consider using CreateSpace. They can print copies for your direct sales, do fulfillment with Amazon, and format and interface for Kindle--all of this, of course, for a cut of the sales. By insisting on "termination at will" contract provisions, avoiding "exclusive" language, and not giving up rights to your work in any agreements, you can change strategies later if you need to contract with other vendors to expand your target market.

The overwhelming trend of self-publishing, which is spurring the publishing business explosion, is also re-shaping it. Your awareness of this allows you take advantage of the opportunities offered by self-publishing while avoiding the downside. A mistake can cripple your ability to share what you created. Study up and be a sophisticated keeper of your work.

Not everyone soliciting your business is a scammer. Legitimate companies have their own brand of hype and often overstate the value of their services. Although their offerings may not be financially sound, they at least deliver what they promise. The problem is that what they promise frequently does not produce the return required to make your investment in what they are selling worthwhile. This is your fault, not theirs. You took the deal.

Run the numbers, be dubious of sales projections, exercise healthy skepticism about programs offered, and remember: **Although it is true that earnings are a function of promotion, the key to selling your book is not what someone else does, it is what you do.**

PUBLISHING STRATEGY: Develop a strategy for turning your manuscript into a book before you begin to reach out to printers or publishers. Define your goals clearly in your mind and don't let the hype take you off track and remember: **If you are fronting the money, a company is primarily out to sell you their services and programs. Selling your book is secondary. They make most of their money from authors giving it to them, not from book sales.** Here are things to consider in order to avoid being scammed or otherwise had as you exploit self-publishing options:

- **Be extremely cautious about giving an agent or publishing company money up front to publish a book.** Giving them money is not how the publishing business works. Those asking for money are most likely vanity publishers, regardless of what they call themselves. In general, it is best to avoid them. Publishers should get their cut when books sell. Any other arrangement gives them a sure profit while you take the financial risk.

- Companies seeking first-time writers to give them their big break are actually seeking the naive to get them to part with their money. Avoid those who solicit your business.

- Royalty percentages are often misrepresented and overstated because of complicated and vague formulas.

- Unless it is a major, established publisher, think twice before letting anyone put their logo on your book. Some experts say it is the "kiss of death," prohibiting your book from being accepted in book stores and causing it to be shunned by serious reviewers. The pay to publish stigma may be unfair, and some argue that it is fading, but it is real.

- Some experts recommend not giving your entire manuscript to anyone, even a reputable publishing company. Instead, send only a couple of chapters. An unscrupulous company can steal your book, perhaps sell it overseas where western books are popular, and you will never know. Or, a publisher might steal your idea and give the book to a writer to rewrite with enough changes that it is no longer yours.

- Be skeptical of promises to get your book in national book stores. Hype about "wholesale distribution" does not guarantee a bookstore presence. There is widespread prejudice against books not published by a major publishing company. Getting your book listed with wholesalers/distributors does not mean book stores will order it.

- Think twice before paying for professional reviews or critique services. These are unlikely to be published in professional venues and the reviewers are not necessarily influential. Such reviews probably won't generate meaningful sales.

- Don't give anyone money to advertise a book unless you satisfy yourself up front that it has the potential to generate enough net cash to you to make the cost worthwhile. In spite of the hype, the likelihood of that is remote. These programs are often overstated and overpriced. Many companies are primarily interested in selling their marketing services to you, not selling your book.

- Before signing any contract, do a financial analysis. Unless you don't care about the financial outcome and just want to throw money out there to get your book published, make certain there is the prospect of a viable return on any money you shell out.

- Don't believe the glory stories of national best selling books, wealth, and fame touted by companies soliciting your business. If the story is true, it is probably distorted and represents an extremely small percentage of writers with whom they do business. Consider the failure rate. A reputable company does not engage in exaggeration to get business.

- Realize that publishing attorneys collect sizable fees for answering simple business questions. Fees can be more than the potential risk. Instead of engaging an attorney, consider eliminating the risk by changing strategy.

- It is standard in the industry for a writer to buy his books from the publisher. In the case of the traditional publishing firms, at least you haven't given them money up front. With others, you may have already fronted the money to print the book, and then you pay to get copies. What is wrong with this picture?

- Investigate any publisher thoroughly online. Look for lawsuits and Better Business Bureau complaints. Google a potential publisher or printer's name and see what comes up. Check them out on the websites *writersbeware.com* and *preditors&editors.com.* Both are venues for reporting scams.

- Maintain control of your product. Don't let anyone else register the copyright. If you are a true self-publisher you will also register the Library of Congress Control Number and ISBN in your name. If someone else does it, they become the publisher of record, not you. Under some circumstances this might not be a problem, but you should understand the consequences, and they should be consistent with your strategy. (It is okay for a graphic designer to create a bar code from an ISBN you purchased in your name.)

- Beware of companies offering to design a book cover. Design quality may be cookie cutter or amateur, and they may own the rights to the cover. You could end up owning the ISBN and the text, but not the cover.

- **Do not sign away the rights to your book. Don't give anyone an exclusive to print or sell it unless you first consult an attorney with experience in publication. Maintain ownership of your work.**

It is important to maintain the right to print and sell your book yourself because selling fewer books direct at a good margin can net you more money with less effort than selling more at a smaller margin through another company.

> With a traditional publisher, you may get a 5 to 15% royalty for each book that sells. An agent can also take a cut. If a book sells for $15, you may net 5%, a whopping 75 cents. In a self-publishing arrangement in which you contract with a company for online sales and another for fulfillment, they may take 55% and 20% of sales respectively, leaving you with a yield of about 25%, or $3.75.

> You've got to sell a lot of books under both of these alternatives to make any money. In contrast, when you personally sell and deliver a book from your own inventory, either through personal contact or your website, you realize about 75% of the $15, or $11.25. The only direct cost you have is approximately 25% for printing and delivery.

This wealth of detail about publishing might make you feel as though you've taken a drink from a fire hose. It is a lot to think about. You may also feel your dream has been trampled and you must go back to watching reality television or take up bowling. Take a break, fill the bird feeder, harmonize in spirit with your dog or cat, file all this information in the back of your mind, and pull it out when you need it. If you narrow your options to CreateSpace, Amazon, and

Kindle you won't need most of this information. Take a look at the website *createspace.com.*

Writers are a sensitive lot, and the hard face of reality may be dispiriting, but we are also a hardy, determined bunch, especially when it comes to sharing what we've created. By educating yourself, you can avoid the hype and pitfalls of those who seek to take advantage of writers' dreams. Become a sophisticated consumer and be thankful for the opportunities the minefield of publication has to offer.

YOUR PROSPECTS: The odds of engaging a literary agent or a major or mid-sized publishing house unless you are famous or an established author are not good. You should be elated if one does accept your book. It means it is a gem. In this business, that is the pinnacle. Being labeled as a published author is huge. There is a downside. It will most likely happen after considerable time and effort, and the publisher will take a huge cut, leaving you very small royalties per book. On the other hand, they have the leverage to generate the sales volume to make it profitable.

Significant time, effort, and cost are involved in trying to engage an agent to champion your book or to get a traditional publishing company to accept it. Considerable work is required to prepare and submit manuscripts, and it is costly.

At $30 a copy and $5 for mailing, you can easily run up over $1,000 in costs, and you may do all this for years and still not get a deal.

A traditional publisher will do the cover design, printing, promotion, and distribution. You will have little control over these processes, and you will be subjected to mandated rewrites. You may not like the cover, and they may change the title. It can take a year or so to get the book out, and you will have little or no influence over the schedule, price, or outcome. This is in contrast to self-publishing where, if you are smart, you control all of these processes.

A publisher may give an author an advance, but don't spend it. This is not the jackpot you might imagine. The writer has to give it back if books don't sell. Major retail book stores and some smaller ones have a policy of returning books that don't sell within a few months.

A book has to sell extremely well for an author to make meaningful money. If a major publisher decides to take your book, they believe in it, and it is most likely a winner. However, they focus on commercially viable books, those that are immensely popular. This narrows the field for most writers who don't fit that mold. Major publishing houses typically show little interest in biographies unless someone famous is involved or you've had something unusual happen to you.

My intent is not to trash the traditional publishers. They are simply seeking a profit. Who can blame them for that? Also, there are so many writers and a limited number of buyers. Simply stated, the supply exceeds the demand. In addition, the mainstream buyer is not interested in what a lot of creative authors write. As proof, look at the top-rated crap on television. A wonderfully intelligent, artful writer's work may not appeal to the masses. Most biographies fit into this category. Mediocre writing is acceptable by a famous person, but others are held to a higher standard. There are a lot of mediocre writers. All this makes a publishing deal a long shot.

In contrast, if you self-publish, you put your energy and money into publishing and marketing the book. You can make it happen, do so quickly, and do it your way. You are in control of the process, and by printing the book yourself and selling direct, the per book profit margin is huge.

LITERARY AGENTS: If you can engage a legitimate literary agent (there are scammers out there), he may be able to hook you up with a publisher, but he will take a 5% to 20% cut of what you make from book sales for the rest of your life. No agent should charge an upfront fee. If they do, they are probably not legitimate. Some are tied into vanity publishing houses.

Their income should be derived from commissions on book sales. Check out agents carefully. Research candidates on line at *writersbeware.com* and *preditors&editors.com*.

> **HINT: A good bet is an agent recommended by a successful author, another reason to join a writers' group or take a class taught by a published author. Also, look in the acknowledgements section of books similar to yours for names of potential agents.**

SELF-PUBLISHING: To use the self-publishing model, you must launch your own publishing company. This involves running a business, which is actually a rather exciting adventure, and forming a publishing company is easier than you might expect. When you get business cards with your publishing company name on it, you are an author and a business person, a double-edged sword for sure, but still an achievement.

Although it is work to self-publish, it may actually involve less effort than you would expend trying to engage a publisher or agent, and you can be certain the outcome is that your book is published. You might also avoid some abuse.

> Publishers can be insensitive. Author Anne Lamott had a publisher's editor tell her she made the mistake of thinking everything that happened to her was

interesting. Ouch! Another author's best selling book was finally accepted by a major publisher after sixty rejections by agents and publishers (representing over $2,000 in submission costs) over a six-year period and after numerous criticisms and mandated rewrites.

All this is avoided when you self-publish. In addition to saving the effort and expense of engaging a publisher, the self-publishing route allows you to get your book out quickly. When you are ready to publish, you publish. You are not repeatedly begging someone to accept your work.

LAUNCHING A PUBLISHING COMPANY: There is no need to form a publishing company if you do not plan to sell your book. Have it printed and distribute it. If you plan to sell it, though, you must move into the arena of publishing in some form.

The prospect of self-publishing is intimidating. You wanted to be a writer and now you are setting up a business, but step by step it is doable, and it puts you in charge of the processes of getting books out. **The good news is that once the publishing setup work is done, you don't have to do it again. You can market your biography through it for years, and you have built the framework for future books.**

If you think you have only one book in you, it may not be worthwhile to form a publishing company, even if you want to sell your book. In this circumstance, go ahead and pursue a full-service vendor. Just be sure you make an educated, thoughtful selection.

Publishing Company Name: "Brand" your author name, not the publishing company name. The company is just a vehicle for getting a book out. That is all it is. Choose a publishing company name that will look good on a book, but one that does not distract from your author name. Don't send up flags that your book is self-published by using your author name for the publishing company or selecting a name that doesn't sound like a serious business. Keep it simple, generic, and businesslike.

Check whether anyone has already registered the name nationally and, if not, register your company. This is done through the Federal website *business.gov.*

Register your publishing company name in your state as well. This is usually done through the county clerk's office and in conjunction with the sales tax application process. They check to see if there is anyone with that name in the state.

By not using your legal name as the publishing company name, you may need to meet DBA (doing business as) registration requirements in your state. The Federal site *business.gov* has information on who to contact in each state to determine registration and DBA requirements.

Don't let these details discourage you. You do them once, and you don't have to do them again. Just get them behind you.

Registering a Publishing Company: After picking a name and registering it with state and federal entities, register the publishing company through the U.S. contracted ISBN Agency. This costs about $125 and is done at R. R. Bowker at *bowker.com*. To self-publish a book, you will do four things through the Bowker company:

   -Register your publishing company.
   -Obtain an ISBN identifier for each book.
   -Obtain a bar code for each book.
   -Register each book.

This is all done online and each of these steps is simple and takes only a few minutes, or maybe an hour or two if you are a technical idiot like me. If you experience problems, Bowker has an email help service and a phone help desk (877-310-7333) where children will help you.

ISBN: This is a unique **International Standard Book Number** that identifies a book, distinguishing it from others. It is on the bar code on the back of books and on one of the first few pages of a book's text, typically referred to as *the publisher's page.* Libraries, book stores, printers, customers, and others in the industry can search for books by this number. ISBNs are available through the Bowker address above.

Each ISBN represents a book. The cost will vary with how many you purchase. You can get one for $125 or ten for $225, which means you can publish ten books before having to purchase more numbers. You can run into problems if you buy an individual ISBN cheaper from vendors who are buying the ten pack and then re-selling. If you market both a printed copy and an eBook, get a separate ISBN for each.

Each time you print a book, you assign an ISBN to it through the Bowker online account created when you registered your publishing company. (You do not have to use a new ISBN for reprints of the same book, however a major rewrite is a new edition and requires a new number.)

Bar Code: When the book's cover is designed, request from Bowker a bar code for the specific ISBN you assigned to the book. Bar codes are used by libraries, book stores, online sales companies, and distribution centers for inventory management and sales reporting. It is a high-resolution graphic that Bowker sends to you (as a TIFF or JPEG file). It is usually placed in the lower right corner of the back of the book. Each bar code will run $35. (If you use a graphic designer, he may be able to create a bar code from the ISBN.) Putting the price of the book on the bar code is optional. If you do so, you can discount the book later, but it is difficult to raise the price once it is on the book, so don't price it too low. More about pricing in *Chapter 10.*

Registering a Book: This is done through Bowker when a book is printed and ready for market. It gets the book listed on the national online *Books in Print Register* which provides your publishing company contact information to the public. You must upload a picture of the book's front cover and a copy of the text.

Registrations are public data bases. Companies that want to sell to you have access to your contact information. They will approach you asking for your manuscript and money. Some are scammers. Even with legitimate offers, you must sell a lot of books to make an investment pay off. As a self-publisher, you are a business person. Use your business head. Calculate what you would realize "net" through any proposals. These companies do many things. The question is: Will those actions sell enough books to make the investment worthwhile?

COPYRIGHTS: A copyright is a symbol of a serious publishing effort, and printing vendors and retail companies expect the copyright and the Library of Congress Control Number (LCCN) to be on the *publisher's page* of a book. However, it is not necessary to copyright a book to protect your rights. Once a book is printed, as of that date you have all rights to it unless you sign them away--something you normally don't want to do. In court the print date typically takes precedence over the copyright date. If someone did steal your work and copyright it, and you have already printed it, the print date takes precedence. Conversely, if they get hold of it and print it before you copyright or print it, they can claim rights to it.

A copyright does not provide protection from someone taking your book and rewriting it. With different wording this is legal (a reason to send only a couple of chapters when submitting manuscripts). It is highly unlikely anyone is going to steal your biography.

To copyright a book, go to *www.copyright.gov*. It is a simple process and costs about $35. You are required to submit an electronic file of the text. Don't let anyone copyright the book for you without consulting with a publishing attorney. **You want to own the copyright in your name.**

The old idea that you can protect work by mailing yourself a certified copy (to establish a date) and not opening the envelope doesn't work. Called the poor man's copyright, this may not hold up in court. It is also unnecessary. Print dates determine when the work is protected.

You cannot copyright the title of a book. Books can have the same title. In those cases the ISBN, author, and publishing company distinguish books from each other. It's a good idea to check if the title you've chosen has already been used.

> **HINT: If you have trouble accessing the *Books in Print Register* to determine whether your title has already been used, do a search of book names on *amazon.com*, *barnesandnoble.com,* and other online and eBook vendors for at least a cursory check.**

LIBRARY OF CONGRESS NUMBER: If you ever plan to sell to libraries, you must have a Library of Congress Card Number (LCCN), also called a Preassigned Control Number (PCN). Other distribution channels may require it as well. You can obtain one free at *www.loc.gov/ publish/pcn/.* Click on EPCN Login. **You probably want the LCCN registered in your name.** Once the book is published, you are required to mail a hard copy to the Library.

PUBLICATION DISCLOSURES: Include in the front of the book a *publisher's page* which provides the publisher, copyright, ISBN, and LCCN information. Include your website address. Study books and note the various formats and presentations. Some have lengthy disclaimers and legal jargon. It is your decision how much to invest in the legal implications of your writing. Believing nothing I write is important enough to attract legal attention, I decided to forgo the legal rhetoric.

CONTRACTS: Be extremely careful about signing contracts or agreements. They are structured to the advantage of the organization writing them. Read the fine print. Understand all terms and conditions. Highlight things you need to study. Google terms you don't understand. I've received printer agreements so complicated that I took the company off my prospect list.

Be savvy when interpreting your percentage cuts. A 25% cut or royalty might look good, but contract language that says your cut is a per cent of "net" revenue as opposed to "retail" means the percentage is applied after discounts, publisher and agent cuts, overhead cost, and who knows what else. (You may never figure out the formula for determining overhead.) These can lower your cut substantially. Base any analysis on net dollars to you, not percentages.

Avoid exclusive provisions, pay attention to qualifiers like "up to" language. It may be important that the contract is time-limited. Make certain you can terminate at will. Note the scope of the contract. It should have clear borders.

Provisions about translating and selling world-wide or granting a publisher the right to feature work in anthologies or compilations can create problems down the road, especially if a major publisher takes an interest in your book. Contract provisions related to these and anything else that is not of value to you should be viewed with skepticism.

If these details about publishing have not dampened your spirit, the next chapter on marketing and distribution probably will, but we are not going to give up. We are on a mission to capture life and to make it so interesting that people will pay to read about it. Marketing is both fascinating and rewarding--another skill mastered. Customize marketing strategy to match your interests, enthusiasm, and what works for your book. Here is how to do that.

Chapter -10-

MARKETING
AND
DISTRIBUTION

The motive for publishing a book is to be able sell it. This is a function far removed from the creative process of writing, but, to share a creation broadly, someone must sell it. A few friends and family members will buy your book to support you, although you will be surprised how many expect you to give them one. You can't count on sales from those you know. I appreciated immensely those who bought a copy, but I also generously gave many away. I mailed them to friends and relatives throughout the country and made a run to Iowa with a box in the trunk. They were a surprise to most. It was a book like any other in a book store--not what most folks expected from an amateur.

You may enjoy marketing a book. If you don't, print a few copies for friends and relatives and pass on publishing and selling. To sell a book, you've got to be committed to do the work to cleverly publish and aggressively market.

> **HINT: Consider recruiting a relative or friend who has a talent for marketing. Also, breaking the work down makes it palatable and delivers steady progress. Try doing one thing each day toward selling. At the end of a month you will have done thirty things.**

Vendors will offer to market your book. They really can't do that effectively. You, as the author, must sell it. Even if you have an agent or a publisher affiliation, you will still be expected to promote sales. When it comes to generating sales, you are it.

MARKETING STRATEGIES: There are several marketing and distribution approaches. Here are key points to consider when determining strategy.

> Direct sales (you do the selling and delivery) are king with the largest profit margin as long as you procure low cost printing.

> Some experts advise writers not to pay anyone to do sales and fulfillment until all other channels with larger profit margins have been exhausted.

Many suggest avoiding the storefront bookstore market altogether and going directly to the online sales channel, which is more expedient, simpler, and more likely to produce volume with less effort on your part.

An even more progressive approach is to go directly to eBooks (electronic books) before marketing through any other channel because of the exploding customer base and the simplicity of this approach. (There is no printing or fulfillment.)

DIRECT SALES: Under the direct sales scenario, you keep an inventory of books and sell and distribute them yourself. (Sales through your own website meet the criteria of direct sales.) This yields the largest profit margin. You incur printing and delivery costs, but no one else takes a cut of the revenue. If you make arrangements with anyone to print or promote your book, you must maintain the right to print and sell it yourself in order to direct sell.

Give flyers and business cards to people you run into who are curious about what you are writing. Be sure your website is obviously displayed on them. Suggest your books as gifts.

HINT: Always have a few books in your car. Put them in a suitcase when you travel.

Book clubs and writers' organizations engage authors to do "readings" at their meetings. Many can be located through an online search. At readings you talk about the book and read excerpts from it. These organizations are composed of readers, a good target market. Still, you are unlikely to generate more than a few sales from this. It's fun, though, sharing what you created with people who appreciate it.

HINT: Put an order form in the book with contact information (email address, phone, and website) so anyone with access to the book can order it. If you have more than one book, you can promote all of them on the order form. Also, through this contact information, people can give you comments about the book. Reader feedback is priceless. Invite input on the order form, at readings, and from anyone to whom you sell a book. (Use these as reviews on future reprints of the book, with permission, of course.)

WEBSITE SALES: Sell direct through your website. Link it to a company like *PayPal* that takes the order from the site, collects the money, and emails you where to send the book. You ship it from your inventory. *PayPal* withholds a small transaction fee for their services and keeps a record of all transactions. They hold money collected from buyers in an account, and you periodically transfer it to your bank. (POD companies are beginning to offer website development and maintenance with payment mechanisms similar to *PayPal*.)

> Setting up a website is easier than you think. I designed one myself with Apple software and support from their trainers. This included a "button" on the site that takes buyers to *PayPal*. Some people won't use PayPal, so put your phone, address, and email information on the website so buyers can contact you direct to order. (If you don't want your personal contact information on the website, set up a business P.O. Box, phone number, and email address.)

A website is only a vehicle for selling direct and for executing the sale. You cannot put it out there and expect sales to happen. No one knows it is there. **You must drive people to the site, and it must be a marketing marvel when they get there.**

> **HINT: Put the table of contents and enticing excerpts from your book(s) on the site. Reviews and reader comments are also good candidates for website topics.**

To set up a website, you must buy the "domain," which is a web address. It costs as little as $20 a year with a discount for purchasing several years. Buy as many years as you can afford. You also need a vendor to connect your site to the web. *GoDaddy.com* is probably the most popular one. Google "website domains" to find others.

HINT: Stay away from companies who put advertising that you cannot control on the site. Read any agreements carefully.

Authors are typically "branded" through their name. The website address name you choose is important. Use your author name if it is not already taken. I selected *www.nikkihanna.com*. I could have used my publishing company name, but people who know me won't necessarily remember the name of a company.

Once you have a domain and a web connection vendor, design the site on your computer with web building software and publish it under that domain. Publishing involves clicking a "publish" icon. Like magic, you are on the web.

The website will require updating periodically. Web maintenance can get expensive if you are dependent on someone else to do it. Once trained in building a site, the maintenance is easy. It involves making changes on the web software and clicking the "publish" icon. Magic again.

You can learn to do this, but if you are not inclined, hire someone to design and maintain the site for you. *Webforauthors.com* is a company that specializes in sites for authors. This can get pricy and, as a result, not cost effective. Perhaps a friend or relative will create and maintain a site for you.

Shipping: Direct website sales require you to ship books. You might think packaging and mailing one is a burdensome process. It is not. Slip the book in a bubble envelope, take it to the Post Office, UPS, or Fedex and send it off. It will cost about $3.50 for the envelope and mail. (If you travel a lot, your unavailability to respond to orders can be a problem.)

SOCIAL MEDIA PROMOTION: Approach this medium thoughtfully, especially with personal relationships. This may be the wave of the future, but many people do not appreciate frequent solicitation of their business on social sites, and you can easily overdo it. As I said earlier, a lot of your personal contacts expect you to give them a book because they know you. When you publish a book, put the word out, but if you mention it too frequently, acquaintances will consider it intrusive. In personal relationships, your being an author is not what you want to be "all about."

Some sites are more business and network oriented than others. Focus your efforts on these. The best way to market through social media is to find an expert and engage him to put the word out to a broad but targeted national market.

HINT: If you notice someone you know showing up in online advertisements that are professional and impressive, contact them and find out who is doing it for them.

As you would do with any other marketing tactic you consider, before embarking on social media marketing, conduct a cost/benefit analysis to determine if expenditures are worthwhile. They may not be.

BOOK SIGNINGS: To say the internet is revolutionizing the book industry is an understatement. Still, conventional marketing approaches can play a role in a writer's promotional portfolio even though, in spite of intense effort, they are unlikely to yield sales volumes comparable to those online or electronic sales channels can deliver.

The book signing approach involves sending notices to newspapers and getting on radio and television, preferably coordinated with a signing at a book store. These activities must be closely coordinated with the media activity occurring just ahead of the book signing. Publicity drives people to the signing.

At first blush, these appear to be grandiose activities, but they are not. They are doable. You may not get on *Good Morning America* or the *Today Show*, but the prospect of your getting on a local television or radio station is pretty good. Odds are you won't get a book signing at a chain like Barnes & Noble, but you can get one at a local book store. You just have to pursue it. If you are serious about marketing, you will do this in many communities. The question is: Do you want to do all that?

Look for book signing locations other than the typical book store setting. Fairs and community events are options. I plan to set a card table up in the street or in a local store at festivals in small Iowa towns and sell autographed copies of *Out of Iowa*. This is a rich targeted market with considerable foot traffic. I have no doubt that over time I will sell all the books in inventory with less effort than book store signings and at a larger profit margin.

At a local book store, the average number of books sold from a two-hour signing is eight. Assuming a book sells for $20, after deducting the store's $8 cut and production costs of $4, an author can score a net profit of $8 a book for a total of $64. Not too bad for two hours.

HINT: You will sell more books at a signing if you have a flyer to hand out that

promotes the book. Information similar to the marketing language on the back cover is appropriate for a flyer. Include a picture and details about other books you've published. Be sure your contact information is prominently displayed.

In addition to promoting the book, this flyer provides an opportunity to engage people in conversation. Stand, rather than sit. (You are not a movie star. They will not come to you.) Try to get a location at the front of the store or other high traffic area. Offer every passerby a flyer, then invite them to take a peek at the book. Have comments prepared that convince them they want to read it.

This is a lot of work, but it can be fun. I know a couple who travel around the country in an RV selling books at book signings. You may be like me, though. I enjoyed my one-time local book store signing. For a couple of hours there, I was an "author" doing what authors do, but it is not something I want to do often.

If you are intimidated about the prospect of being on TV or radio and find a book signing awkward or too much work, you have something in common with the majority of writers, who tend to be an introverted bunch. You don't have to do it. Don't do anything that takes the fun out of your writing experience.

RETAIL BOOK STORE CHAINS: It might surprise you to learn this is not a lucrative market for most writers. National retail book stores rarely buy self-published books, and vanity books are shunned. Also, most of these stores demand huge discounts and have an unattractive return book policy whereby books are returned for a refund if they don't sell in a few months.

Further, their purchasing protocol requires that they obtain books through wholesalers/distributors. You can't walk into a store and get them to buy your book. Without the muscle of a major publisher, it's hard to get into the large retail stores, but you may not want to market through them anyway. Their discounts, return policies, and rigid procurement practices make the alternatives of selling through online or electronic book channels more attractive.

LIBRARIES: Like national book chains, libraries tend to shun self-published books and have standard acquisition protocols involving specific distributors. I dropped a couple of my *Out of Iowa* books off at libraries in Iowa and it seemed to pretty much befuddle the staff. They had no way to pay for them, so I donated them. You might explore the library market after you've tapped the more lucrative online retail and eBook opportunities. Optimally apply your energy and time to the channels with the most potential. Libraries may not be a priority.

LOCAL BOOK STORES: Although national book stores with established purchasing protocols may not take your book, local retail book stores tend to be supportive of local authors. They will buy a few books or take them on consignment when you drop into their stores, although this is unlikely to be a high volume sale. They might even schedule a signing and run an ad in the paper to announce it. This brings people into the store. Just remember: **Getting a book into a book store does not mean it will sell. You've still got to steer people to the store to buy it.**

LOCAL RETAIL STORES: A biography set in a geographical area is of interest to people in that area. Local gift shops, museums, tourist shops, cafes, and coffee houses might buy your book for resale.

It is a stretch to expect that all of the above activities together will generate the sale of 100 books. This reflects the formidable prospect of selling the 200 book average. These methods are how marketing has historically been done, but the industry is evolving. Now there is the internet, which has changed everything.

ONLINE SALES: When a book is listed online, it can potentially pop up on a computer screen anywhere in the world when someone does a search. The prospect of that happening depends on the online marketing plan you chose, the key words on the book cover, and the categories in which the book is listed. To get the best exposure, purchase a couple of books on selling online and study them. Strategy can make all the difference when it comes to online sales.

Still, how well your book sells depends primarily on the intensity of your marketing efforts. To beat the average sales of 200, you must execute a calculated marketing strategy and, to make any money on these sales, you must do so at minimal cost. Going directly to Amazon with no middleman and understanding the programs it offers should yield the optimum net income. If you do need a vendor for fulfillment, consider CreateSpace which is owned by Amazon.

Amazon is the primary online sales channel at this time, and it offers several approaches to selling, each with its own pluses and minuses. To your benefit, this company's marketing strategy is brilliant. If you've bought books from them, you have observed the customer side of that effort. Still, you are the key to generating sales, and your ability to select the optimal Amazon plan for your book and to get people to the site will determine the level of success. Buy a couple of books on how to sell on Amazon and become informed. (Buy them through Amazon so you know what your customers will experience.)

Amazon will take a cut, ranging somewhere from 20% to 55% depending on the plan you choose. They may discount the book, which can influence your ability to sell direct at the retail price. It might also cannibalize your direct sales, which have a larger profit margin.

High sales volumes must be realized on Amazon if you are to make a meaningful profit. This requires that you understand the plan you select and work the marketing machine to the max.

You can use a POD company, to fulfill Amazon book orders, or you can skip the middleman and ship books to Amazon yourself from your inventory. You will need to print, store, package, and ship books, but these tasks are not arduous. (You are doing this for your website sales anyway.) Amazon will probably want to maintain an inventory of approximately twelve books. You can easily box and ship books to maintain that level. If you travel a lot, supplying books in a timely manner can be a problem, and this option is probably not right for you.

HINT: Many POD vendors and vanity publishers imply that you must use them to

get a book on Amazon. This is not true. You can do it yourself. Buy a book that tells you how and work your way through the process. It is doable, and it might be the best plan for you.

Even if substantial sales are not realized through Amazon, it may be important to you to know the book you created is listed on the primary online retail source of books in the world--Amazon. Being an author is not all about sales volume and money. It is about creating something and sharing it. It may also be about being recognized as an author. Having a book listed on Amazon will do that for you, maybe more so than having it sold in a book store.

ELECTRONIC BOOKS: Some argue that paper books are headed for the niche market. Whether that proves to be true remains to be seen. Although it is unlikely that beloved printed books will go the way of the VHS tape, there is little doubt that the future is in eBooks. To get a book on an electronic reader, it must be formatted for that medium and then electronically connected. There are companies that do this for a fee and/or a cut of the earnings. Smashwords.com is one of the largest. If you are using CreateSpace for digital printing and fulfilling Amazon online sales, it is an easy step to have them format a book for Kindle for around $100, and have Amazon sell your electronic book along with the printed one. Make certain you understand the formula for calculating what you will net per book when using any formatting service.

Be cautious of POD and vanity publishers who suggest connecting you to an eBook retailer for a hefty price and try to lock you into a deal that can limit your options later. You can avoid the middleman altogether by doing the reformatting yourself and supplying the electronic files. However, the formatting requirements are complicated. In keeping with the business concept of more profit with less time investment, a more optimal approach is to spend your time on promotion or perhaps on writing another book and let someone else do the tedious formatting.

Optimal pricing strategies for electronic book sales are still evolving. Most eBook buyers are price sensitive and books typically sell at a price less than the printed copy because of competition. The retailer will probably set the price by discounting. There a sweet spot between $.99 and $4.99 which is popular. This sounds low, but there are no printing, inventory, or distribution costs. Still, the profit margin is low, especially if you are sharing revenue with a vendor who is formatting and connecting you with an eBook retailer. When a book sells for a couple of bucks, your cut per book is minuscule. However, with a good book and your fierce marketing, the potential to make meaningful dollars through high volume sales is there.

The promise of the eBook market is alluring. Dipping your toes into this pond could change everything. If you are serious about marketing a book, designate a month to study up, become an educated consumer, and give it a shot. YOU can do it. How exciting is it to think your book is on electronic readers like Kindle and the iPad?

SALES PROMOTIONS: Produce flyers, bookmarks, and business cards to mail to prospective buyers or to insert in books when you send them out. Build a contact file, send emails, and make social media postings to announce when a book is published and how to order it. Emphasize your website on all these promotional materials and prominently display it on your book. Also, include the book's ISBN.

> **HINT: Promote your book in October as a Christmas gift. In the spring, suggest it for Mother's Day or Father's Day.**

You may do all this and still be challenged to achieve the average sales figure of 200 books. Generating substantial sales requires a full court press of marketing techniques. If you want to do that, study how to market books and dig in.

HINT: Set marketing priorities. Test online and eBooks channels through approaches that require minimum investment. Exhaust methods that deliver the biggest profit margin before trying others. You have limited energy and money. Put it into optimal prospects--the ones most likely to deliver the goods.

The reality might be that there is not a large market for your book. For biographies this is often the case. That's okay if you define success this way: You created it, put it out there, and those who read it enjoyed it. Perhaps your memoir is a stepping stone to another book which has a broader market.

PRICING: Pricing the book is a critical process. When selling direct through your website, a book may sell better if you set a lower price and add a handling fee. Pricing a book at $16 with a $3.95 handling fee can generate more sales than pricing it at $19.95 with no fee. (It is difficult these days to sell a book for more than $19.95.)

Most books, whether in book stores or online, are discounted by the retailer. You have no control over this. A book retail priced at $12.99 might be discounted to $6.99. It will face keen competition from similar books, and buyers are price sensitive. Discounting is strategically smart. Most sellers do it. The important thing for you to know is whether you are paid your percentage based on the discounted sales price or the retail price.

HINT: Check prices of competitive books in a book store and on Amazon before pricing your book.

You can have a price printed on the bar code, on the back of the book, or not at all. There is controversy over which way to go. Don't price too low. Whether you are paid based on a percentage of the retail or net price, the highest retail price you can set while still being competitive with other books is probably the most optimal. It is a balancing act.

Be aware that there is a Federal Trade Commission (FTC) regulation requiring that any deal you make with one customer be offered to all like customers. The operative word here is "like." Different discounts for different categories of customers are allowed as are discounts based on volume.

FULFILLMENT: Some sales will be to people with whom you have direct contact. In this case, fulfillment is simple. They give you money; you hand them a book. Sweet. When you begin receiving orders through your website, mail, and email, you must distribute the books. You can order a book from your POD vendor and have them ship it to the buyer, or you can fulfill from your own inventory. The post office book rate, called media rate, runs about $2.41 for a 280-page softback book in a bubble wrap cushioned envelope which costs approximately $.75. If you contract with a vendor for fulfillment, you eliminate the inventory, packaging, and shipping functions; however, if you are in the majority who sell 200 or fewer books, there is no substantial challenge to distributing books yourself, that is unless you travel a lot.

DEFINING MARKETING SUCCESS: As a writer, marketing might not be your forte, but it is the avenue by which your creation is broadly shared. The extent to which you do that is up to you. It is tempting to get swept away with the hype and define success by the number of sales, but you are successful as an author when you produce a book. Whether it is shared broadly or narrowly, you did it. It exists.

When you first hold a copy of your newly printed biography, reflect on the fact that you created something, a legacy no less. Consider the void that would have existed had you not produced it--a life story gone forever. Your book is out there for generations to come--preserved for posterity. That is success beyond measure. Whether it sells a little or a lot, it was shared.

Chapter -11-

BUSINESS ISSUES

If you don't sell books, you don't have to deal with business issues, and none of the information in this chapter applies. When you cross over into selling them, you are essentially running a business and all that that implies.

BUSINESS OBJECTIVE: You must decide whether you want to focus on writing for pleasure or for profit. The elusiveness of profit has been suggested. Earnings may or may not be realized. The pleasure, on the other hand, is almost guaranteed. At any rate, consider what your goals are from a business perspective. They will drive many of your decisions.

BUSINESS STRUCTURE: When setting up a publishing company, keep it simple. Set it up as a sole proprietorship unless there is a compelling reason to do otherwise. Consult an accountant or lawyer if you need advice on the structure.

BANK ACCOUNT: You should open a business bank account in your publishing company name and run all transactions through that account. For tax purposes it is important to keep personal and business transactions separate. Also, people will make checks out to your publishing company and without an account in that name, you will have trouble cashing them. Checks made out in your name can be deposited into the business account with no problem since you are the signatory.

CREDIT CARD: A business credit card keeps charges separate from your personal card.

BUSINESS CONTACT POINTS: You can set up separate phone, P.O. Box, and email contact points, perhaps in your publishing company's name. Whether you do that or not depends on how serious you are about the scope of your business and your sensitivity to privacy.

ACCOUNTING: The likelihood of making enough money to make a profit, at least initially, is remote. However, you must track revenue and costs and report them for tax purposes. Most likely the costs will exceed the revenue and you won't owe income tax on what is sold. In fact, you can take a loss for three years, but after that the IRS and state income tax commissions expect a business to show a profit or they disallow the losses on the premise that the business is a hobby. When you reach this point, you can still deduct costs up to the amount of revenue to avoid income taxes on that revenue, but you can

214

no longer take a loss. You may need a tax expert to guide you through the tax maze.

HINT: Factor the impact of income taxes into calculations when projecting net money earned on books.

BUSINESS TAXES (SALES TAXES): Whether realizing a profit or not, if you sell books, you are required to pay local city or county sales taxes, sometimes called transaction taxes or business taxes. In many states you pay none if your book was sold through the web or to someone out of state; however, this situation is fluid. States are passing laws to capture that tax revenue, perhaps by applying use tax laws.

Register your business with the local tax commission or franchise board, most likely at the county court house, and comply with any business tax requirements. You will get a permit number which identifies your company.

HINT: When you order books printed for direct sales, understand your state laws. You may not be required to pay sales tax on that order, but rather you will pay the tax when you sell the book

FEDERAL EIN: Businesses are required to have a Federal Employer Identification Number. That name is a misnomer because you must have one whether you have any employees or not. It is IRS form SS-4. You can call 1-800-829-4933 to get a number. Anyone who sends you money may require the EIN in order to report to the IRS any money disbursed to you. Some state sales tax commissions require the EIN as well.

At this point, you may feel overwhelmed. When the business requirements of self-publishing hit me and I discovered all I had to manage in order to sell books, it was too much and I gave up. I wanted to write books, not run a business. However, over time, these things gradually got done, step by step. One month you build a website, the next month you hook it into *PayPal*, the next you register your business, get an EIN, and open a business bank account. Every few weeks you accomplish another business task. A few months later, the business is in full swing, the steep learning curve is behind you, everything is set up, and you are off and running.

Don't let the business tasks kill your dream. Once many of these things are done, you don't have to do them again. Time spent is an investment which will pay off over and over in the future. You have built the base. You are in business.

Chapter -12-

A LIFE CAPTURED

A Gift Given, a Legacy Created

There is an immense reservoir of wisdom out there which few people recognize and even fewer tap into--the wealth of experience generated from a life fully lived. When that life is gone, precious treasures of a uniquely magnificent story are lost forever if not captured in some manner. Writing that story is a tangible, expressive, and enduring way to make a life matter now and in the future to who knows how many generations. This is no little thing.

Many life stories are not written because people believe they cannot write. The primary goal of this book is to dispel that notion, to provide the tools and perspective to give everyone the confidence to know they can turn their life or someone else's into a unique, relevant, and beautiful story. YOU can do it. **You can write.**

It is important throughout the creative and often tedious process of producing a biography, or any other book, to understand why you are doing it and to judiciously guard and protect that objective.

> Define success on your own terms. If you define it as everyone loving and buying your book, you may be disappointed. If you define success as having produced the book and shared it with whoever is interested, then success is inevitable. In the case of a biography, you are sharing a life and leaving a legacy. That alone is success. You can feel good about that.

To ensure that you enjoy the process of creating a biography, consider a flexible, fluid time frame for doing all that is required to make it happen. Set soft dates rather than hard ones and liberally adjust timelines as necessary to avoid stress. Take things step by step.

> Embrace tasks in increments of months. Gradually your progress will generate significant results. When overwhelmed, focus on what has been accomplished, not what must be done. Relish the process and revel in the personal growth it produces. Then explore what amazing progress can be accomplished in the next month, and the next, and the next.

There are many nuances to producing a captivating life story that portrays vividly the essence of a person. To the novice biographical writer, that means there is a lot to learn. Don't let learning or anything else delay getting started with the actual capturing of the story. Write. Interview the players. Make these two things a priority. Life is fleeting, yours and that of others. Avoid the regret of delaying the chronicling of it. Allow yourself to do some shabby writing and just do it, story by story. The polish can come later as learning builds.

Share your writing journey as you go along. The joy a person experiences when they see their life in print suggests a sense of urgency to get as much as possible down on paper in draft form, even though the final product is not there yet. Generate drafts of stories to share with others, particularly if you are writing about them. Involve them in the process. Don't miss the opportunity to create the joy of relevance for someone. Don't wait to publish after the life is over so you can write the final chapter. You can always write the ending later.

A clear sense of purpose will fuel the determination and persistence required to produce a captivating biography. My wish for you is that you find a sense of purpose that will carry you through the process--a reason for capturing life. Approach it in whatever manner works for you--simple and concise or full out. Either way, make it a biography that when it is discovered in an attic generations from now, the person making the discovery holds it in his hand and says out loud: "Wow!"

ACTION PLAN
CREATING A BIOGRAPHY

This list of action steps may be intimidating, but remember the actions can be spread over several years. Do a few things each month and consider what your world will be like when the creation comes to fruition--a legacy is born. During the development process, be on a continuous quest for a story and write. Always write.

--GETTING STARTED--

_____**Define Purpose, Vision, Frame of Reference, and Tone**. Why are you doing this? What do you want to accomplish? How do you see it affecting others? How do you feel about it yourself?

_____**Identify Audience.** Who are they and what do you want them to think and feel when reading the story?

_____**Define Success.** Do you aspire to simply create something and share it with whoever is interested, or to become a writer by profession? Is success being a publisher and a business person? Do you have to sell huge volumes of books and make money to feel successful?

_____**Determine Strategy.** Are you going to take the simple route of writing, printing, and distributing your biography or are you going to go all out and publish and sell it?

_____**Develop Learning Plan.** Take writing courses. Attend seminars. Read books about writing and publishing. Research author blogs online. Join a writers' group.

_____**Interview People.** Inquire about events, personalities, connections, and daily life. Look for tidbits and hooks. Probe. Focus on the feelings around events. Verify dates, facts, and details.

_____**Collect Photos.**

_____**Take Professional "Author" Picture for Cover.**

_____**Set Up Place to Write.**

_____**Set Up a Place in Which to Drop Reminder Notes**

--WRITING--

_____**Create First Draft.** Regurgitate. Get it all out. Create a comprehensive first draft (not to be published). Save it in both electronic file and hard copy form.

_____**Copy First Draft to a Working File.** Create a file to use for development of the book.

_____**Set Up Outtakes File.** Writing taken out of the working file goes into this file.

_____**Review Working Draft.** Move narrative that does not make the cut to outtakes file.

____**Organize text.** Develop *table of contents*. Use it to move text into logical locations in the manuscript.

____**Identify Themes.** Identify and understand major themes of a life--the perspectives that drive choices.

____**Establish Structure.** Organize beginning, middle, and end. First paragraph says what book is about. Last tells how things turned out. First paragraph of a chapter tells what it is about. Last paragraph transitions to next chapter. String stories together. Balance intensity and humor through book to avoid weak chapters.

____**Do Run-Throughs:**
___**Develop characters.** In depth portrayals.
___**Describe environment.** Background, settings, scenes, details of the times.
___**Build out stories.** Write story by story. Use layering, tidbits, defining moments, and rebel jewels.
___**Interject historical events.** Relate personal experiences to historical incidents.
___**Make minor events major ones.** Round out incidents with detail and perspective that shape them into colorful occurrences.
___**Add dialogue and quotes.**
___**Enhance word selection.** Look for more interesting, colorful, and descriptive words. Use a thesaurus.
___**Add sentiment.** Paint a picture of feelings, passions, and connections with people, animals and nature. Interject perspectives of others--how they view the world.

___**Apply reader perspective.** Remove self-indulgent comments and write for the reader.

___**Introduce humor.** Add humor and repeat humorous themes throughout the manuscript.

___**Repeat references to key life events.** Show how these create impact throughout life.

___**Tighten up wording.** Don't state the obvious. Remove unnecessary words and redundant sentences and paragraphs.

___**Create transitions.** Improve flow from word to word, sentence to sentence, paragraph to paragraph, and chapter to chapter.

___**Thread.** Run threads of life's themes throughout book. Repeat key points. Make references to jokes or drama again in different context. Tie back and tie forward.

___**Write in Active Voice.**

___**Remove/replace pronouns.** Eliminate "I," "me," "you," and "your" where appropriate.

___**Replace or remove weak words.** Search for stronger words. Eliminate "very," "really," and words ending in "ly" where possible. Use words like "some," "all," "would," and "could" frugally.

___**Eliminate distracting and nonessential words.**

___**Improve every sentence.** Focus on structure and effectiveness of words. Put strongest sentences at beginning or end of paragraphs.

___**Ensure that all sentences and paragraphs have relevance.** Each one should be humorous, touching, interesting, convey a lesson learned, or contribute to another paragraph. Eliminate redundancies.

___**Look for words to emphasize.** Use italics, bolding, quotation marks. (Don't overdo.)

___**Enhance format.** Add white space, break up paragraphs, indent to emphasize paragraphs, and create lists.

___**Take a break.** Let the manuscript bake.

___**Read out loud.** Concentrate on flow, transitions, sequences, story continuity. Resolve awkward wording.

___**Review spelling, punctuation, grammar.** Question suspect words, review punctuation marks for appropriateness and consistency, check for grammar errors.

___**Seek independent edit.** Have someone else proof--a fresh set of eyes.

___**Share drafts.** Seek feedback.

___**Read from the perspective of others.**

___**Read pretending you are your worst critic.**

___**Read for fun.**

___**Repeat run-throughs as appropriate.**

--MECHANICS--

___**Establish Computer Backup Capabilities.**

___**Develop Technical Skills.** Take courses or seek a trainer. Learn formatting, graphic design layout, file transmission, and web building or recruit someone to do these things.

___**Format Text.** Establish book size, set margins, spacing, fonts, headers/footers, page numbering system, chapter breaks and headings.

____**Develop Photo Incorporation Skills.** Learn to scan and digitally load photos, adjust and enhance them, assure 300 DPI resolution, add captions, and inline into text.

____**Develop Proofreading/Editing Skills.** Study proofreading technique. Engage another person to proof.

____**Establish Source for Grammar/Punctuation Rules.** Select style book source and an online search engine.

____**Establish Source for Spelling Rules**. Use spell check, search engine, thesaurus and dictionary.

--COVER--

____**Layout/Graphic Design.** Recruit a friend or relative with technical design experience, find a professional source, or learn to do it yourself.

____**Determine Title, Subtitle, Hooks.**

____**Design Cover (front, spine, and back).** Use layout software if producing book. If putting in notebook, can do on text software.

____**Determine Cover Content.** Seek input from someone with marketing background.

____**Insert Author Photo and Short Bio.**

____**Consider Including Reviews.**

____**Proof.** Have another set of eyes look at cover.

--PRINTING--

____**Study Printing Industry**. Understand traditional, POD, and vanity publishing. Avoid scammers. Do cost benefit analysis on any services offered.

____**Determine Volume.** Print a small number of books for the first printing.

____**Decide Digital or Offset.**

____**Determine Marketing/Distribution Model and Sales Channel** (self-sell, print on demand, online, or some combination).

____**Determine Print Bid Specifications.**

____**Identify Printer Prospects.** Check them out on *writersbeware.com* and *preditors&editors*.com.

____**Solicit Quotes.**

____**Review Printing Contract Detail.** Don't agree to give up rights. Don't give anyone an exclusive to print or market. Don't let a printer put their logo on your book if you are self-publishing.

____**Select Printer.**

____**Determine file transmission requirements (Typically PDF format).**

____**Submit Files.** Send text and cover files for proof.

_____**Review Proof and Submit Changes.**

_____**Prepare for Shipment Delivery/Storage.**

****

If you do not intend to sell the biography and are simply producing it as a gift for friends and family, many of the following action steps do not apply.

****

--SELF-PUBLISHING--

_____**Determine Publishing Strategy.** Study publishing business. Avoid scammers. Consider cost benefit of alternatives. Reassess. Ask yourself: Do you really want to publish and sell?

_____**Name Publishing Company.** Check state and national registries to assure name not taken.

_____**Determine Price of Book.**

_____**Register Company** with *Bowker.com.*

_____**Purchase ISBN** at *Bowker.com.*

_____**Purchase Bar Code** from *Bowker.com.*

_____**Register Book** with *Bowker (myidentifiers.com).*

_____**Copyright Book.** Submit electronic copy.

_____**Obtain Library of Congress Number (LCCN).**

--MARKETING AND DISTRIBUTION--

____**Study Book Marketing.** Read books, online blogs, research options.

_____**Determine Marketing Strategy.**

____**Develop Direct Sales Plan.**

____**Assess Online and eBook Opportunities.**

____**Develop Promotions.** Flyers, emails, social media, bookmarks, business cards, inserts.

____**Develop Website.** Determine site name and obtain domain. Design site and publish it.

____**Install Payment Process on Website.** PayPal or some other mechanism.

____**Arrange Signings and Media Promotions.**

____**Contact Book Clubs and Writers' Groups.**

____**Publicize.** Contact friends and relatives. Use social media. Promote book as gifts.

____**Marketing Services.** Before procuring marketing services, do cost/benefit analysis and check vendors out on *writersbeware.com* and *preditors&editors.com*.

--SET UP BUSINESS--

____Engage Accountant.

____Determine Business Structure

____Set Up Bookkeeping Processes.

____Set Up Business Contact Points. PO Box, business email and phone (all optional).

____Open a Business Bank Account.

____Obtain Business Credit Card.

____Meet County/State Requirements. Business license, sales tax registration, DBA (doing business as) filing. Each state is different.

____Obtain Federal EIN. Employer Identification Number (needed for tax purposes).

____Set Up Sales Tax Payment Capability.

____Calendar Business Requirements/Tax File Dates.

____Mail Copy of Book to the Library of Congress.

____Throw a party to celebrate your book.

--EXAMPLES--

FIVE WRITING TECHNIQUES
(Excerpts From *Out of Iowa*)

Technique 1 - Break it Down
Write Story by Story

My next running amuck experience occurred when I took a road trip to California with Donna Mae, who was moving there...Her dog, Toby, made the trip interesting because it was too hot to leave him in the car so we had to eat all our meals at drive-throughs, and because he had to pee. I placed him down among the cacti to do his business in the Mojave Desert. There was no grass to be found. He started dancing around pretty good on the hot sand, so I picked him up and held him a few inches above the ground, shaking him gently to induce him to pee, which he had not done since Prescott, Arizona. He was way overdue. Toby looked back at me like: "What the hell are you doing?" I finally gave up and tossed him in the car, telling Donna Mae we needed to get out of here pronto. "We must find grass," I said in a tone of severe desperation, which caused her to give me a strange look until I explained Toby's dilemma.

Toby can be temperamental. Perhaps that is an understatement. When I'm unable to reach Donna Mae by phone, I worry that Toby has eaten her. She walked him late every night before we went to bed, which concerned me somewhat but not enough to miss my favorite television show, so I didn't accompany her one evening. As she was leaving the hotel room with an overenthusiastic Toby in tow, I asked her, "If you don't come back, can I have your car?" (*Out of Iowa*, p. 25)

Technique 2 - Apply Layers
Start with Facts and Layer on Details and Feelings

At any rate, the crisis rallied my folks to my side, and they spent time in Oklahoma giving me support. They realized that if they didn't, they could lose me. It was a scary and puzzling time for them. I recall sitting on the couch beside Mom and crying so hard that she started rocking me. She held me and rocked me for hours. I finally slept with my head in her lap, her stroking my hair. I felt like a child. (Thirty years later, she would do it again.) How difficult that must have been for her...

I was so afraid and felt like I was fighting a raging battle all day every day. I was trying so hard to make it. When the therapist suggested I give up the fight, I was shocked. "Give up," he said, "Just lean into it. Flow with it." Giving up was such a strange concept to me, but he maintained that if I would just chill and let things play themselves out, I could cope better. He was right.

I let go and began taking things as they came rather than trying to solve all the problems in my world. This was an important lesson, and I've used this "giving up the fight" approach to coping throughout my life. Sometimes we just try too hard...

I moved into a one-day-at-a-time approach to things while keeping my eye on becoming independent and providing for my family. For awhile it was all about survival, but gradually I began thinking about a serious career and "the good life" for my children. I began to think about the prospect of life being fun. (*Out of Iowa*, pp. 141, 142)

Technique 3 -Mine Tidbits
Embellish the Details

As Grandma Go Go, I have my limits when it comes to childrearing. I get overwhelmed pretty easily, particularly when there is more than one toddler involved. You know you have too many whelms when you leave Cheerios from breakfast and peas from lunch on the floor as a later snack for a foraging toddler, when you give up on snapping every other snap on children's clothing and don't snap any at all, when it becomes okay that a child is wearing something backwards or wrong side out, when you have given up plucking your eyebrows and shaving your legs is not even on the radar, when it doesn't occur to you to make your bed even if company is coming, when you are taking morning vitamins at bedtime if at all, and when it becomes irrelevant that you are wearing clothing backwards or wrong side out...

While simultaneously playing an alphabet game and trains with my three year old sidekick (we were multi-tasking), I had an out-of-body experience. I was floating around the room observing myself saying: "Come on over here little s, and big R you need to scoot over there." Meanwhile, a train circled on a track around my butt. This event occurred after singing several choruses of a song about sitting in a high chair banging a spoon, running toy cars through a car wash, hiding in a cardboard box that smelled like, well, like cardboard, and performing a chemistry experiment with Fruit Loops. It was pure, unmitigated craziness, and I loved it, which proved I had lost my mind, therefore, the out-of-body experience.

The revelation was not over yet. My floating-around-the-room self began answering questions from my on-the-carpet-in-the-middle-of-a-train-track self. The question was: "Is this a big W or a big M?" The answer, of course, was: "It can be whichever one you want it to be." Later while pondering letters d and b, my out-of-body self realized I was in a loop while my other self was busy responding to a squeaky voice complaining that my butt was on the track blocking Thomas the Train. I have too many whelms. (*Out of Iowa*, pp. 201, 202)

Technique 4 - Discover Defining Moments
Write About What Changed Everything

For some years, Mel and her sophisticated, jet-setting friends flew all over the place for business and fun--New York to ring the bell at the stock exchange, Vegas for Halloween, Tampa for New Years, and Trinidad for Carnival, etc. Then, in her mid-thirties, motherhood happened, and that changed everything. She is now settled in California with her little family and our shopping strategy has shifted. We used to doll up, be looking good, and shop and dine at marvelous places. Now we shop separately while one of us is home with the toddlers, or we divide and conquer, each of us taking a child. We don't dress up nice anymore. I usually look like a bag lady with a human appendage. My shopping venue is the nearest dollar store where the objective is finding the diaper aisle and locating a toy lawn mower while managing a toddler who does not want to move past the gum machine. As for dining in marvelous places, that ain't happening unless Chuck E Cheese qualifies. It is a sad, sad, sorry situation. (Out of Iowa, p. 167)

Mom never accepted the fact that medicine could not fix everything. She was determined to get to the bottom of the matter and asked a doctor for the umpteenth time what was wrong with her ears. In frustration he said, "YOU CAN'T HEAR." The eye doctor also told her she couldn't see, and sadly she was sitting around waiting for the next thing she couldn't do. Soon she was unable to walk, and that changed everything...We went someplace every day--*Thelma and Louise* heading out on some small adventure, but the days of big adventures were behind us. I could tell she was declining. The medical crises began gaining momentum. I tried to get her mentally prepared for the impending nursing home stage of her life, but, as is often the case, she had difficulty accepting the inevitable. Mom went into a nursing home at eighty-eight...It is a struggle when, as she said, "You can't walk so good, can't hear so good, can't see so good, and are no good." She did have some vitality left as evidenced by her being in trouble with the staff for speeding in her wheelchair...(*Out of Iowa*, p. 117)

Technique 5 - Expose Rebel Jewels
Include Rascal Behavior and Bold Departures

It was scary to watch him race. I was frequently in the stands with his fans. During the warmup lap, when he passed in front of the stands, he always gave us the "thumb up," and everyone hooted and hollered. I would say: "He's so cute," which tickled his friends. I was anxious before the race, but once it started I could get into it...The deathly quiet in the stands after a wreck where he was knocked senseless paralyzed me, but eventually the "thumb up" came out of the car window, the crowd roared, and I could breathe again.

Marty was always a fearless risk taker, which I find both fascinating and terrifying. He is a fireworks aficionado and once rappelled down a high rise building for a charity event. I watch his antics when I can, going to drag races, stock car races, pool tournaments, or whatever, always recognizing that it is his world, and I am just visiting. Sometimes I was more a part of his world than I bargained for.

I dropped my new car off at his shop to have him tint the windows, and he gave me a loaner. Little did I know it was one of his drag cars-- revved up, rocking, and ready to roll. I sat at the end of the driveway, waiting for a break in traffic, and when I got it, I pressed the pedal and peeled out, fishtailing all over the place. I was thinking: "Wow!" However, I still had not grasped the magnitude of the situation.

Idling at a red light down the street, I noticed how loud it was. Chug, chug, chugging away, and bouncing. The frigging car was bouncing. I glanced over at a man in the car next to me who was clearly amazed that an old woman was driving this hot rod. Then it died. I mean it just coughed it up and frigging died. I started it back up, turned around, and headed back to the shop. When I walked in, Marty and his friends were rolling with laughter. "Hey, Mom, if you need more power there is nitrous in the trunk." Humor at my expense was common among them, and I played my role, pitched a fit, and left with a suitable car. (*Out of Iowa*, p. 160)

ABOUT THE AUTHOR

Nikki Hanna has a B.S. Degree in Business Education and Journalism and a Master's Degree in Business Administration. A retired Certified Public Accountant and Toastmaster, she has many years of experience at various levels of management in the business community. She has played key roles in merger and acquisition ventures, been a consultant for national industry task forces, and served on the board of directors for numerous corporate and charity organizations. Nikki has served as an advisor on curriculum development for educational institutions and on strategic planning for charities.

Now an author and keynote speaker, Nikki is dedicated to enlightening aspiring leaders and encouraging the capture of life stories through biographical writing. She lectures at colleges and universities on management and leadership and promotes biographical writing through her books and speaking engagements.

Nikki speaks about leadership, woman's issues, aging and retirement, and biographical writing. She is available for educational sessions and entertainment programs for professional, charity, book clubs, senior groups, and women's organizations. Comments on this book are welcome at neqhanna@sbcglobal.net.

www.nikkihanna.com

TO ORDER

AUTHOR: Nikki Hanna

Available: Amazon, Kindle, or www.nikkihanna.com

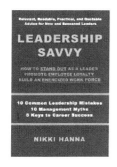  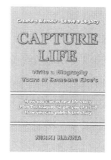

NAME_____

ADDRESS_____

CITY_____STATE_____ZIP_____

PHONE_____EMAIL_____

Quantity_____ *Leadership Savvy* - $19.95
Quantity_____ *Out of Iowa* - $19.95
Quantity_____ *Capture Life* - $14.99

To Order by Mail: Send check to:
Patina Publishing
727 S. Norfolk Avenue
Tulsa, Oklahoma 74120
To Order by Phone: 918-587-2451
To Order by Email: neqhanna@sbcglobal.net
To Order from Website: www.nikkihanna.com

Details about educational programs, entertaining speeches, and book readings on biographical writing, leadership, aging and retirement, and women's issues are available. Discounts are provided for volume purchases of books. Comments on this book are welcome at the above contact points.

19823442R00129

Made in the USA
Charleston, SC
13 June 2013